LIBYA

TITLES IN THE MODERN NATIONS OF THE WORLD SERIES INCLUDE:

Afghanistan	Kenya
Argentina	Kuwait
Australia	Lebanon
Austria	Liberia
Bolivia	Mexico
Brazil	Nigeria
Cambodia	North Korea
Canada	Norway
Chile	Pakistan
China	Panama
Colombia	Peru
Congo	Philippines
Cuba	Poland
Czech Republic	Russia
Denmark	Saudi Arabia
Egypt	Scotland
England	Somalia
Ethiopia	South Africa
Finland	South Korea
France	Spain
Germany	Sudan
Greece	Sweden
Guatemala	Switzerland
Haiti	Syria
Hungary	Taiwan
India	Thailand
Iran	Turkey
Iraq	United Arab Emirates
Ireland	United States
Israel	Vietnam
Italy	Yemen
Japan	
Jordan	

LIBYA

BY DEBRA A. MILLER

LUCENT BOOKS

An imprint of Thomson Gale, a part of The Thomson Corporation

THOMSON

GALE

Detroit • New York • San Francisco • San Diego • New Haven, Conn. • Waterville, Maine • London • Munich

X 916.12
Miller

On cover: Pedestrians and cars pass beneath an archway in Tripoli, Libya's capital.

LIBRARY OF CONGRESS CATALOGING-IN-PUBLICATION DATA

Miller, Debra A.
  Libya / by Debra A. Miller.
    p. cm. — (Modern nations of the world)
  Includes bibliographical references and index.
  ISBN 1-59018-443-2 (hard cover : alk. paper)
  1. Libya—Juvenile literature. I. Title. II. Series.
DT215.M55 2005
961.2—dc22
                                                                    2004017962

Printed in the United States of America

CONTENTS

INTRODUCTION

A Former Terrorist State?

Throughout its early history, Libya, an oil-rich Arab nation in North Africa, was ruled by larger powers. It finally declared its independence in 1951, shortly after the end of World War II. Libya's current leader, Muammar Qaddafi, came to power several years later in 1969 when a military coup ousted King Idris, the nation's first leader. As part of Qaddafi's revolutionary ideas that were formed in reaction to Libya's experiences with repressive outside rule, Libya's new government committed itself to helping revolutionary groups around the world fight against oppressive regimes. Qaddafi in particular sought to oppose nations such as the United States and Israel, which he believed wanted to dominate weaker countries or peoples through military might and economic intimidation.

Beginning in the 1970s, Libya established ties with dozens of revolutionary groups and terrorist organizations that were fighting Western powers and their allies. Qaddafi's government hosted foreign terrorists and trained them at special camps on Libyan soil. The nation also sold arms to various rebel organizations and granted asylum to terrorists wanted by other countries. Libyan diplomats even supplied terrorists with intelligence on possible targets, forged documents, and provided assistance in arranging safe houses in the target countries. A large part of Libyan aid went to Palestinian groups that conducted terrorist attacks against Israel, but Qaddafi was also linked to various other insurgent groups and radical governments in Europe, South America, Asia, and South Africa. Qaddafi sent Libyan troops to provide military instruction and other help to some of the groups he sponsored. For example, Libya sent troops into the neighboring country of Chad in 1980 to support the rebel army in that country's civil war.

In addition, Libya became directly involved in perpetuating terrorism by conducting military attacks on Libyan dissidents abroad and by commissioning terrorist acts to be carried out either by Libyans or by other terrorist organizations. Libya was suspected of being involved, for example, in a 1984 killing of a policewoman in London as well as the 1986 bombing of a discotheque in Berlin that killed two U.S. servicemen and one Turkish civilian and wounded more than two hundred others. Also, six Libyans were convicted by a French court for the 1989 bombing of a French airliner over the Sahara Desert in Niger. That deadly act killed 170 passengers. Perhaps the most publicized Libyan terrorist attack, however, was the December 1988 bombing of a Pan American airliner over Lockerbie, Scotland. The explosion caused the plane to crash, killing all 259 passengers and 11 of the town's residents. A Libyan intelligence officer was later convicted of the murders.

Libyan leader Muammar Qaddafi has actively supported terrorist groups since seizing power in 1969.

Because of its support for terrorism, Libya was the subject of U.S. and international trade sanctions for almost twenty years. These sanctions crippled the Libyan economy and, many believe, ultimately led Qaddafi to moderate his radical foreign policies. In 1999 Qaddafi's government began to accept responsibility for the Lockerbie crash, agreeing to pay full compensation to the victims of the tragedy. In 2003 Libya even volunteered to give up its programs to develop weapons of mass destruction, including chemical, biological, and nuclear weapons. Libya's actions, in turn, led to the lifting of United Nations (UN) and U.S. sanctions as well as to renewed economic relations between Libya and Western countries.

The optimism shared by leaders around the world as a result of Qaddafi's apparent change in policies, however, was dampened in June 2004 when it was reported that Qaddafi may have promoted a 2003 covert terrorist operation to assassinate the ruler of Saudi Arabia. Months later, the investigation of this incident has yet to be completed, and there is no consensus about Qaddafi's true intentions. Many hope, however, that the era of Libyan terrorism has truly ended so that the nation can take its rightful place within the international community.

1

A DESERT LAND

As part of northern Africa, Libya lies just across the Mediterranean Sea from Italy and Greece. Its northern border is a beautiful 1,000-mile coastline, and its other borders are shared with several countries: Tunisia and Algeria to the west, Niger and Chad to the south, and Egypt and Sudan to the east. Libya occupies a large territory of 679,358 square miles, making it the fourth largest country in Africa and about one-fifth the size of the United States. Although it is fortunate to have some coastal areas where people can live and grow crops, most of Libya is arid desert. Its true economic riches come from underground in the form of oil and gas reserves.

LIBYA'S THREE REGIONS

Libya has three distinct geographical regions: Tripolitania, Cyrenaica, and Fezzan. These areas are different geographically, and they developed as completely separate provinces.

Tripolitania is located in the northwest corner of the country, along the Mediterranean Sea. It is known for its coastal lowlands and is marked by coastal oases, sandy beaches, marshes, and lagoons. Although Libya has no permanent rivers, these coastal areas contain numerous wadis, or riverbeds, that fill with water during the rainy season as water rushes toward the sea. Moving inland, the land rises into a triangular plain called the Jifarah Plain, which is framed by the sharp mountains of the Jabal Nafusah, reaching heights of about three thousand feet. The Jabal Nafusah are made of limestone and are believed to be the sites of ancient volcanoes. Today, however, they are dry and largely barren of vegetation.

Tripolitania's coastal plains contain some of Libya's most fertile agricultural land. Various crops are grown here, and numerous trees have been planted to produce citrus, dates, almonds, and olives. This area is also the location of Libya's capital city, Tripoli, and the region where the majority of Libyans live.

Cyrenaica, the largest of the three regions, is found in northeastern Libya and is the country's other coastal area. It is separated from Tripolitania by Sirtica, a stretch of barren wasteland desert that extends northward along the Gulf of Sidra. Like Tripolitania, Cyrenaica contains some coastal lowlands that stretch out in a crescent shape. Cyrenaica's coasts contain fertile soil used for growing grapevines and fruit trees. Many people live in several port cities located on the coast, including Benghazi, Libya's second largest city. The

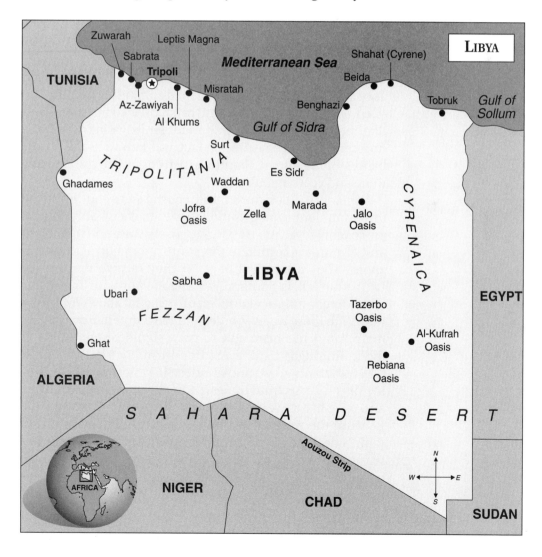

region's lowlands are bordered by the Marj Plain and a mountain range called Jabal al-Akhdar, or Green Mountains. These mountains are the greenest and arguably most beautiful place in the country. They support forests of pine, juniper, cypress, and olive trees. From these mountains, Cyrenaica stretches southward into the vast Sahara Desert.

Libya's third region, the Fezzan, lies inland, south of Tripolitania, and forms the northwestern part of the Sahara Desert. Huge sand dunes, stretches of gravel, rocky plateaus, and an occasional oasis can be found here, but little else.

COASTAL RICHES

Libya's breathtaking Mediterranean seacoast is a narrow strip of land that runs the length of the country's 1,075 miles and abuts the broad Libyan Desert. This coastal fringe, although small in acreage, provides a bounty of blessings such as beaches, fish, harbors, and a mild climate for farming. Indeed, since ancient times, settlers have fished the shores and dammed up the wadis to trap water for irrigating crops. The northern African coastline, in fact, was known as the breadbasket for the Roman Empire, which controlled the area two thousand years ago.

In modern times, these fertile coastal areas continue to be important for farming. Although they make up only about 2 percent of Libya's total land area, coastal areas in Tripolitania and Cyrenaica comprise the country's major agricultural zones. They are prized because they receive the bulk of Libya's rainfall. In addition, the Jifarah Plain near Tripoli has an underground water aquifer, or well, that allows for irrigation. With these water sources and the temperate coastal climate, Libya has been able to grow significant amounts of food. Although it still must import many food products, Libyan farmers grow various crops, most notably wheat, barley, olives, citrus fruits, dates, peanuts, and vegetables. They also raise livestock such as goats, sheep, cattle, and camels. Because the water levels in the underground systems are rapidly declining from intensive agricultural and urban water usage, however, large quantities of water are now pumped to the coast from underground water reserves located below the southwestern desert.

The coastal areas also provide fishing grounds for Libya, although its waters are not as productive as other Mediter-

A Libyan vendor displays fruit for sale at a market in the coastal city of Tripoli. Libya's fertile coastal areas comprise the country's principal farmland.

ranean countries because of low levels of plankton, the microscopic nutrients eaten by many fish. Most of Libya's fishing industry is located on the western part of its coastline, near Tripoli. Yet one of Libya's most lucrative fish products, sponges, is harvested in Cyrenaica. Since ancient Greek times, area fishermen have monopolized sponge fishing, using equipment that allows them to fish in deepwater beds where the best sponges can be found.

Sunny Mediterranean beaches, pristine with fine white or golden sand, are another rich gem found in Libya's coastal areas. Libya has recently begun to encourage tourism here. A number of resorts can now be found on Libya's coast offering first-class accommodations and a chance to experience the nation's beauty.

LIBYA'S DESERT

Libya's most prominent geographic feature, however, is the immense desert that makes up most of the country's landmass. As journalist John K. Cooley puts it, "Most of Libya's 679,358 square miles is a sea of sand, dust, and rocky hills."[1] Indeed, Libya's deserts are part of the great Sahara Desert that covers most of northern Africa. The Sahara is the largest desert in the world. It stretches well beyond Libya and measures close to one thousand miles north to south and at least three thousand miles from east to west, an area about the size of the continental United States.

The Sahara was once a green and lush landscape that provided a home to many plants and animals. Thousands of years ago, the area slowly changed and dried up. Today, hot winds continue to rise and fall over the desert, pulling away moisture and rarely allowing any rain. The desert's defining characteristic, therefore, is extreme dryness.

The Sahara, however, is more than just a sea of sand; it has a variety of landscapes. Sand dunes make up only about 15 percent of the desert, but these dunes can be quite impressive. A dune known as the Libyan Erg, for example, is as big as France. The rest of the desert consists of rocky plains covered with stones and gravel, occasionally broken up by shale and limestone plateaus and mountain ranges. The desert also contains a number of oases, areas with underground wells and springs that provide enough water to support trees, grass, and sometimes crops and small villages. These oases have been used for centuries as rest stops for nomads who wander the deserts looking for grazing areas for their herds of animals. The rest stops also allowed for trade between the ports of North Africa and markets farther south. Without oases, crossing the desert would be virtually impossible.

Some of the biggest oases are located on huge subterranean aquifers that hold great quantities of water. Two of

Part of northern Africa's immense Sahara Desert, the deserts of Libya make up most of the country's landmass.

the most well known are the one beneath the Al-Kufrah Oasis in southeastern Cyrenaica and another near the oasis community of Sabha in the southwestern desert. Libya dug wells at these sites in the 1970s to harvest the water for agricultural use at the oases. The government's most ambitious effort to utilize this water, however, began in the 1980s with the Great Man-Made River Project. This monumental project taps the aquifers at Al-Kufrah, Sabha, and another oasis (Sarir) and transports the water through huge pipelines to the larger coastal agricultural and industrial areas.

For centuries oases like this one have provided shade and water to nomads who wander the Libyan desert with their herds.

CLIMATE

Libya's position between the Mediterranean Sea and the Sahara Desert produces dramatically different climate zones. Because of the cooling ocean waters, the coastal lowlands enjoy a Mediterranean climate, with warm summers and mild winters. Temperatures average about 86 degrees Fahrenheit in summer and about 46 degrees in winter. This area gets most of Libya's rainfall—about fifteen inches per year—which falls mainly in the winter months. This rainfall can be erratic, sometimes producing droughts that can last for a couple of years. The cooling moisture from the ocean also brings high humidity. In the nearby highlands and mountains, temperatures are colder, sometimes reaching the freezing point, and snow is possible.

The desert areas experience a strikingly different climate. The Sahara is one of the hottest places on earth. Temperatures there can rise as high as 136 degrees Fahrenheit in the summers, and even in the winter temperatures average about 60 or 70 degrees. Desert rainfall is very light, and as in other parts of Libya, the amount of rainfall varies greatly and is punctuated by severe droughts. Sometimes it rains in the desert as much as four inches per year, but other times as little as a fraction of an inch of rainfall. Even in the wettest

THE OLD TOWN OF GHADAMES

One of Libya's most interesting cities is Ghadames, a town with about ten thousand people located in the heart of the desert at an oasis near the borders of Tunisia and Algeria. It has been called the "jewel of the desert" because of its natural beauty, important monuments, and distinctive architectural style. Once an important stopover point for trade caravans crossing the Sahara Desert, Ghadames survives today as a small agricultural and camel-breeding center and as a location for Libyan military training. The small city is mostly known, however, as an example of ancient architecture perfectly adapted to the desert climate. In the older part of the town, all the houses are white and made of mud, lime, and palm tree trunks. They are constructed to fit closely together, with covered alleyways that allow people to walk easily from one place to another. This construction provides excellent shelter from the

summer sun and heat. Indeed, although most Ghadames residents have moved into newer housing in the town, they often return to the old village in the summertime to escape the heat. The town is also a recommended site for tourists, both for its interesting architecture and as an example of early Libyan culture.

A whitewashed, covered walkway in the ancient city of Ghadames offers shade from the sun.

parts of the desert, it may rain twice in one week and then not rain at all for several years.

With such dry conditions, desert sandstorms are common, especially in the spring and fall. These storms are driven by great winds called the *ghibli*. They create a wall of quickly moving, extremely hot, dry air and sand that can rise thousands of feet high. The *ghibli* appear with no warning and can last from a few hours to several days, until they abruptly stop. Often, they blow into the coastal towns, damaging crops and making it difficult for people to see or breathe.

Plants and Animals

Despite its mostly harsh desert climate, Libya has a variety of plant and animal species that have adapted to its challenges. Along the coast and in the oases, vegetation is the typical Mediterranean mix of olive, fig, palm, and citrus trees. On the plateaus and higher areas, trees such as fir, juniper, and cypress grow. Farther inland, one finds expanses of flat, dry grasslands that produce an abundance of wildflowers in the springtime.

As these grasslands give way to the desert, however, the dry sand and rocks support little vegetation other than an occasional plant called camel thorn and microscopic plants that sometimes wait years for a bit of rain that allows them to grow for a day or two. In the deserts, most plants are found in the oases, where water is available. Here, the date palm grows, along with figs and decorative plants like oleander.

Even though it is mostly desert, Libya is home to many animals. A variety of migratory birds can be seen throughout Libya, as well as some nonmigratory species such as larks, partridges, prairie hens, raptors, and vultures. In the desert regions, small animals occur, including the desert hare, red fox, hedgehog, and several types of rats. The camel is the most visible large desert animal, although other large species, such as hyenas and herds of antelopes and gazelles, were once common. Lizards, snakes (some of which are poisonous), and scorpions are also quite numerous.

Libya's Population

Based on 2004 estimates, the people of Libya number about 5.6 million, five times the population size reported in the first

Libyan census in 1954. The population increased rapidly because of a high birthrate and the government's encouragement of large families, which it believed were needed to meet Libya's labor needs and to fuel economic development following the country's discovery of oil. The result is that the current population is overwhelmingly young; the median age is about twenty-two years old.

Ethnically, most Libyans (97 percent) are a combination of Arab and Berber stock. The Berbers, a distinct seminomadic northern African people with their own Berber language, were once the dominant culture in the area. Arab nomads from the east, however, migrated to North Africa centuries ago, bringing with them Arabic language and culture and the religion of Islam. Today, these groups have intermarried and only a few ethnically "pure" Arabs and Berbers are left in Libya. Most Libyans regard themselves as Arabs, and most speak Arabic and practice Islam.

Libyan men and women walk through a market in downtown Tripoli. Most Libyans regard themselves as Arabs and most practice Islam.

Libya is also home to about 160,000 foreigners, mostly from Tunisia, Pakistan, Turkey, Sudan, Syria, and India. Because of its small population and workforce, Libya has needed to import foreign workers to help run its oil industry and develop its economy. In the 1970s this group swelled to one-third of Libya's total population, but in recent years, Libya's declining economy has caused the government to order many nonessential workers to leave the country.

Other Libyan ethnic groups include small numbers of the Tuaregs, another nomadic desert tribe; black Africans who are the descendants of former slaves; and two virtually extinct ethnic groups—the Tebu and the Duwud. The Tebu are a small, dark-skinned people from Libya's southern deserts who speak a language related to Nigerian. The few remaining Duwud, also dark-skinned, live in western Fezzan.

Two European ethnic groups who once lived in Libya have largely departed. A number of European Jews established colonies in Libya early in the twentieth century, but in the 1940s most left to take up residence in the newly created Jewish state of Israel. Also, before Libya's 1969 revolution, a sizable Italian community resided in Libya, left over from when Italy ruled the country. Most Italians, however, left Libya after the revolution.

A Tuareg nomad poses with his camel in the desert of the Fezzan region.

LIBYAN CITIES

Because of Libya's dry climate, the Libyan people tend to live in communities near the coasts or in desert oases where water can be found. The population, therefore, is mostly urban and concentrated largely near the two main coastal cities: Tripoli, the country's capital in Tripolitania, and Benghazi, located in Cyrenaica. Several smaller urban areas ring the capital city, such as Misratah (on the coast east of Tripoli), Al Khums (also on the coast east of Tripoli), and Az-Zawiyah (on the coast west of Tripoli). Other urban centers include Tobruk (in the northeast), Sabha (in the desert south of Tripoli), and Beida (on the coast northeast of Benghazi). These urban areas have grown rapidly in recent decades as rural people and nomads have migrated to the cities to find jobs and a better standard of living. Unfortunately, this influx of people has also contributed to overcrowding, a lack of housing, and a drain on social services.

One-fourth of Libya's population, or about 1.89 million people, live in Tripoli, an ancient city in northwestern Libya near the Tunisia border. Hundreds of thousands more live in the sprawling metropolitan areas surrounding the city. Many of Tripoli's buildings in its oldest sector, called the medina, were built centuries ago by the Turks when the Ottoman Empire ruled the area. The city also has an Italian section, built during that country's rule; it features wide avenues, large buildings, parks, and residential areas. The older parts of the city are known for their lush gardens filled with olive trees, palms, grapevines, and orange groves. Today, Tripoli is Libya's largest city, a major seaport and commerce center, and a place of industry. Thus in the more modern part of the city one finds government buildings, tall apartment buildings, public housing projects, and industries having to do

A major seaport and a center of industry, Libya's capital city, Tripoli, is the nation's largest and most developed urban center.

with oil refining, textiles, and food processing. Tripoli is also the site of Al-Fatah University, several museums, a technical university, and a few embassies.

Benghazi, Libya's second largest city (with over 1 million inhabitants), is another very old city. Located on the Mediterranean in northeast Libya, it is the main port and urban center in the Cyrenaica region. Benghazi was virtually destroyed by bombs during World War II, but since then it has been rebuilt into one of the most attractive cities in North Africa. Modern buildings complement wide, open spaces. It is also a major center for agriculture and various industries, from oil refining to sponge fishing, and is home to a university called Gar Younis.

The ancient architecture of Tripoli's medina offers a sharp contrast to the high-rise buildings found in the modern section of the bustling metropolis.

OIL RESOURCES

Once one of the poorest countries in the world, Libya now is one of the richest, due to the discovery of oil deposits in 1959. Libya's crude oil is a high-quality oil that contains less sulfur than oil from other parts of the world. This makes it cleaner and cheaper to use and therefore very desirable in the world market. As a result, Libya is Africa's major oil producer and one of Europe's biggest North African oil suppliers. In fact, Italy, Germany, Spain, and France purchase 74 percent of Libya's exports. Libya has proven reserves of 29.5 billion barrels of oil and a production capacity of 1.4 million barrels per day. It also has some largely undeveloped natural gas reserves. In addition, much of Libya's territory remains unexplored, leaving open the possibility of finding and developing additional oil and gas resources.

Most of Libya's known oil reserves are located onshore in three main areas: in western Libya at the Samah, Beida, Raguba, Dahra-Hofra, and Bahi oil fields; in the north-central

THE GREAT MAN-MADE RIVER PROJECT

Because Libya consists mostly of desert, the majority of its people live in a narrow coastal strip near two major cities, Benghazi and the country's capital of Tripoli. Development, agriculture, and population increases in these areas have depleted coastal underground water supplies. As a result, Libya began work on a huge project in 1980 to tap vast underground water reservoirs in the desert and carry this water through large pipelines to the coast. This project, called the Great Man-Made River Project, is the largest water transport plan ever undertaken. Many have even called it the eighth wonder of the world. Its total cost is expected to be about $30 billion.

The desert water reserves are located in four enormous underground basins in southern Libya. More than one thousand wells have been dug into these basins to pump the water, and more than three thousand miles of con-

crete pipeline, some thirteen-feet wide, have been laid to transport it to coastal cities. The first stage of the project was completed in 1994 and provides 2 million tons of water each day to Benghazi; the second phase, finished two years later, provides similar water resources to Tripoli. Most of the desert water is expected to be used for agricultural development, which will help Libya produce more of its own food. The underground water, however, is only expected to last for about fifty years.

A crane lowers sections of an enormous water pipeline into place as part of the world's most ambitious water-transport project.

part of the country at the giant oil fields at Defa-Wafa and Nasser, and a large gas field at Hateiba; and in the east at the Serif, Messla, Gialo, Bu Attifel, Intisar, Nafoora-Augila, and Amal fields. Twelve of these onshore oil fields have reserves of 1 billion barrels or more, and two have reserves of more than 500 million barrels. Libya also has some offshore oil deposits; the largest is located at El Bouri, which has proven reserves of at least 2 billion barrels.

Libya's economy is tied almost exclusively to oil, and there are few other industries of any significance. In fact, oil exports account for as much as 90 percent of Libya's revenues. At current production levels, however, Libya's oil may last for only another forty years. If the state fails to find more oil or develop other industries, the economic future of Libya may be as dim as it was before its oil boom. Even when the country's oil is flowing, declines in world oil prices can cause serious economic difficulties for the nation. Diversification of the Libyan economy, therefore, is an important issue for the country.

Before oil was discovered, agriculture provided about a quarter of Libya's gross domestic product and allowed Libya to export food. But agriculture has not kept pace with the country's growing population, and now Libya must import food to feed its people. Also, agriculture as an industry is limited by the small amount of land able to be cultivated (about 2 percent of Libya's total land area) and by the country's lack of water resources, resources Libya's government has been criticized for failing to properly conserve. For these reasons, agriculture has not developed into a viable alternative source of income for Libya.

Similarly, Libya's industrial capacity has not grown significantly since the discovery of oil. Despite massive government investments in industries such as textiles, electrical machinery, milling, and food processing, these industries have suffered from numerous problems. Among these problems are inferior product quality, corruption, a lack of resources and markets, and insufficient numbers of skilled workers. In the 1980s and 1990s, falling oil prices, economic sanctions imposed on Libya by the United States and the United Nations, and the government's expulsion of many foreign workers further threatened Libya's efforts to develop its economy. Libya's main resource and source of income, therefore, continues to be oil.

2 Libya's Many Cultures

Libya was formed from three separate ancient cultures, giving it cultural diversity and at the same time producing stark divisions between various regions. It also has been ruled by many different powers, as a result of a series of invasions by neighboring tribes and other outsiders. The nation of Libya emerged as a truly independent and united nation only after the discovery of oil provided it with economic resources.

Libya's Early History

Archaeological evidence, such as prehistoric paintings and carvings of animals found on rocks, suggests that the area now called Libya was inhabited as early as 8000 B.C. Some of these early inhabitants farmed or raised cattle on the coasts. Others lived a nomadic life as herders and hunters in a well-watered grasslands landscape in what is now the Sahara Desert. Writer Geoff Simons notes how different Libya looked in prehistoric times: "In what was to become the largest desert in the world [ancient artists] drew clear pictures of elephants, giraffes, crocodiles, rhinoceroses and many other creatures. There was water in abundance for the hippopotami and for the trees whose fossils have been found in parts of the desert where trees no longer grow."[2] As the climate changed and the grasslands turned to desert, most of these herding and hunting cultures disappeared.

Around 3000 B.C., a tribal people called the Berbers migrated to the area now known as Libya. The Berbers are somewhat of a mystery to archaeologists and historians. Although no one knows for sure where they originated, they were Caucasian and spoke a language with Afro-Asiatic roots. Some evidence suggests that they came from southwestern Asia and slowly extended their range to northern Africa. The Berbers first settled in Egypt and later moved into Libya.

Centuries later, Libya's location at the crossroads between Europe, central Africa, and the Middle East made it attractive to outsiders as a trade center for slaves and other merchandise. This brought an influx of new peoples to Libya.

THE PHOENICIANS IN TRIPOLITANIA

The first known traders to come to Libya were from the ancient land of Phoenicia, which was located in the eastern Mediterranean area of modern-day Lebanon and Syria. Even before the twelfth century B.C., the Phoenicians developed trade relationships with the Berbers in the Tripolitania region and built trading posts on the Libyan coast. By the fifth century B.C., the Phoenicians' trading empire dominated northern Africa. Based in a city called Carthage (in modern-day Tunisia), the Phoenicians created the distinctive Punic civilization in North Africa. The ancient Punic cities of Sabrata, Oea, and Leptis Magna, for example, were located in an area that became known as Tripolis (meaning "three cities")—the site of today's city of Tripoli.

An ancient cave painting depicts animals that thrived in Libya in what was once expansive grasslands but is now desert.

Tripolis became a strong maritime power. Its sailors and merchants traveled around the Mediterranean to trade in ores, spices, and other produce. The Phoenicians also brought a knowledge of agriculture to North Africa and established extensive farms on Libya's coastal plains. It is said that they introduced olives, grapes, peaches, and figs to Libya. In addition, the Phoenicians traded with the Berber tribes who lived farther inland, creating good relationships between the two groups. Indeed, the Berber tribes absorbed many of the Punic customs and learned to speak the Punic language.

As the Phoenicians expanded their trading activities in the Mediterranean, however, they increasingly threatened the largest power of the day—the Roman Empire. A confrontation between these two peoples in the Punic Wars finally led to the defeat and destruction of Carthage in 146 B.C. Thereafter, the area around Tripolis became a Roman province called Tripolitania.

GREEK INFLUENCES IN CYRENAICA

The Roman ruins in the ancient Phoenician coastal town of Sabrata date to the first and second centuries.

The eastern Libyan coast—the region now called Cyrenaica—was first colonized by Greek traders. Greeks from the island of Thera migrated to the North African coast and founded the city of Cyrene in 631 B.C. Other Greek cities followed, including Berenice, which later became known as

The ruins at Cyrene serve as a testament to the magnificence of the city that the ancient Greeks established here in 631 B.C.

Benghazi. Like the Phoenicians in Tripolitania, the Greeks developed this part of Libya as an important trading and agricultural center. The Greeks introduced new crops, raised large herds of sheep and cattle, and traded in barley, corn, olive oil, apples, saffron, and an ancient (now extinct) plant called silphion, which was used both as food for cattle and as a medicine for humans.

For a century, the Greeks of Cyrenaica resisted numerous outside attacks by Egyptians from the east and Phoenicians in the west. In 525 B.C., however, Cyrenaica was conquered by Cambyses, son of the king of Persia, and the area lived under Persian rule for two centuries. Finally, in 331 B.C., Alexander the Great arrived to oust the Persians and again impose Greek rule. Cyrenaica continued under Greek rule even after

Alexander died in 323 B.C., at which time it was divided among his generals.

Greek influences made the region a center of both wealth and culture. Indeed, Cyrene became one of the greatest educational and artistic cities of the Greek world. It was known for its medical school, academic centers, and fine Greek-style architecture. In 74 B.C., however, Cyrenaica, like Tripolitania, became a Roman province when it was bequeathed to Rome by the last Greek ruler, Ptolemy.

THE INDEPENDENT FEZZAN TRIBES

While the coastal areas were being colonized by the Phoenicians and the Greeks, the desert areas of the Fezzan region of Libya remained largely independent, dominated by the Garamentes, a powerful and wealthy desert tribe. The Garamentes were traders who controlled the desert caravan trade routes from central Africa to the Mediterranean. They were hired by the Phoenicians to carry goods such as gold and ivory from the Sudan to their ports on the coast. They also controlled caravan routes eastward to Egypt and westward into Africa.

Little is known about the Garamentes, except for the information gleaned from archaeological sites. Some researchers believe they were part of the Berber tribes, while others think they were related to another tribal group, the Tuaregs. Evidence shows that the Garamentes were based in a string of western oases, controlled by a capital called Gerama. At these oases, the Garamentes irrigated portions of the land for agriculture, built impressive towns made of stone, and became skilled horse breeders and cattle herders. Archaeological digs also found that they constructed more than fifty thousand pyramid tombs.

Although the Romans colonized the coastal areas, they never succeeded in controlling the tribes that inhabited the interior parts of Libya. The Garamentes were strong enough to resist repeated attempts by Rome to eradicate them. Finally, in the first century A.D., Rome formed a commercial and military alliance with the Garamentes, who then thrived as traders for several more centuries.

ROMAN RULE

Tripolitania and Cyrenaica remained Roman provinces for more than four hundred years. During this period, the two regions prospered, sharing a European culture—the Latin language common throughout Greece and Italy, the Roman legal system, and Roman identity. Cities and towns flourished, and the two regions exchanged goods along protected

LEPTIS MAGNA: LIBYA'S RICH ARCHAEOLOGICAL SITE

The land now called Libya was ruled in ancient times by a variety of powers, including the Phoenicians, the Greeks, and the Romans. This rich history has left Libya with some of the most important archaeological sites in the Mediterranean. One of the most attractive of these sites is Leptis Magna, which contains the remains of a large Roman city. Located near Tripoli and founded by the Phoenicians in the tenth century, Leptis Magna was once a bustling port city where the Phoenicians traded slaves, gold, ivory, and precious metals, surrounded by rich agricultural lands. Later, the city came under Roman and then Arab control, until it was abandoned to the desert sands in the eleventh century. Finally, in the twentieth century, it was excavated, revealing many archaeological and architectural treasures. These include large marble- and granite-paneled Roman baths, massive religious shrines and arches honoring Roman gods and rulers, forums and museums, and a magnificent Roman amphitheater, where chariot races and other events were once held.

A huge amphitheater is one of the many architectural treasures uncovered at the Roman settlement at Leptis Magna.

roads and sea routes. Tripolitania became a major olive oil exporter and a trading post for gold and slaves shipped to the coast by the Garamentes. Cyrenaica blossomed as a producer of wine, drugs, and horses.

In A.D. 70 Cyrenaica's destiny was suddenly changed when it became home to tens of thousands of Jews. They were sent there by Rome after the Romans destroyed Jerusalem during a rebellion against Roman rule in Palestine. In 115 the Jews in Cyrenaica revolted once again against the Romans. Although this uprising was also thwarted by the Romans, the fighting destroyed much of Cyrenaica, especially the city of Cyrene. It took Cyrenaica another hundred years to recover and return to prosperity. During this time, Christianity was introduced within the Jewish community, and by the end of the fourth century it had spread throughout Rome's North African provinces. Under late Roman rule, therefore, Libya became a predominantly Christian region.

Roman power was finally weakened in the fifth century A.D., when the Vandals, a warlike tribe from Spain, invaded northern Africa and established a stronghold in Carthage. From there, the Vandals raided Libyan cities and demanded that businesses pay them taxes. These acts of extortion severely damaged the prosperity of the region. The Vandals were eventually defeated by the armies of Belisarius, a Byzantine general who in 533 began to take back northern Africa for the Roman Empire. The old Roman order and glory, however, could not be restored. Although the coastal regions continued under Roman rule for another century and a half, they never again rose to their previous level of wealth and high culture.

THE ARAB INVASION

Roman rule gave way to Arab rule in the seventh century as a result of the birth of a new religion called Islam, which was founded by the prophet Muhammad in the Arabian Peninsula. The followers of Islam, called Muslims, believed in one God ("Allah") and sought to bring all of society under Allah's will. After Muhammad's death in A.D. 632, Islamic armies carried the message of Islam from Arabia into northern Africa. By 642 Omar Ibn al-As, an Arab general, conquered Cyrenaica. Two years later, he moved into Tripolitania, establishing control over that area within a decade. In 663 the Arabs invaded the Fezzan region, conquering the Garamentes' capital of

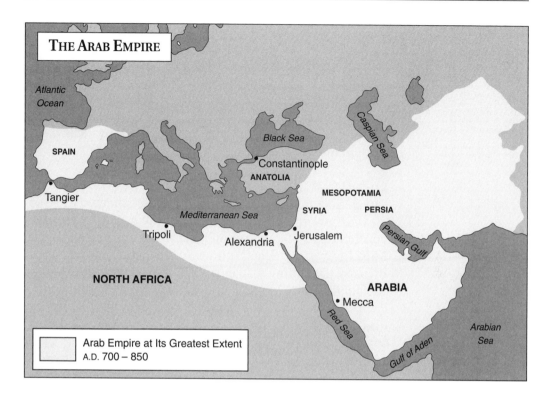

THE ARAB EMPIRE

Atlantic Ocean

SPAIN

Tangier

Black Sea

Constantinople

ANATOLIA

MESOPOTAMIA

SYRIA   PERSIA

Caspian Sea

Mediterranean Sea

Tripoli

Alexandria

Jerusalem

Persian Gulf

NORTH AFRICA

ARABIA

Mecca

Red Sea

Gulf of Aden

Arabian Sea

Arab Empire at Its Greatest Extent
A.D. 700 – 850

Gerama. Although the Berbers initially resisted Islam and staged numerous rebellions against Arab rule, most of these tribesmen eventually embraced the new religion. By the eighth century, Arab rule was firmly rooted in northern Africa.

The Arabs established a political system throughout the Middle East in which religion and politics were united under a caliph, a supreme Islamic religious leader. Northern Africa was governed by a succession of emirs, or commanders, who were subordinate to the caliph. In addition, the region was subject to a legal system based on Islamic law, or sharia, which was administered by religious judges called *qadis*. All other loyalties, including tribal and family loyalties, ranked second to Islam.

This new system of Islamic and Arab rule succeeded in northern Africa largely because Arab warriors intermarried with native peoples. Early Arab invaders were followed by even larger waves of Arabs who were moved into the region in 1049 to put down a revolt by the Berber tribes. As political analyst Lillian Craig Harris recounts, "This time it was not [Arab] warriors alone who moved, but entire tribes—up to

200,000 families entering North Africa via Egypt within a few months time."[3] Over time, these tribes spread throughout the coastal areas and into the Fezzan, displacing the Berbers and taking over their traditional lands. This invasion slowly and firmly embedded the region with Arab culture and the Islamic religion. Over the next few centuries, almost everyone became a Muslim and the area of today's Libya was transformed into an Arab land.

OTTOMAN RULE

The period of Arab rule, however, was also marked by struggles for power among the Arabs. In the seventh century, a conflict regarding who should rightfully be the caliph split Muslims into two sects, Sunni and Shia, and spawned a Shia dynasty, the Fatimids, in Egypt. Later, the Fatimids extended their control into Libya. Eventually, however, Fatimid control crumbled and Ottoman invaders conquered first Cyrenaica and then Tripolitania, making both areas part of the Ottoman Empire by 1551.

Although Ottoman rule lasted for nearly four centuries, it was threatened by numerous revolts and was never fully established in the interior of Libya. The Ottomans ruled largely through military force and repression. They established large military garrisons in Libya's coastal cities and taxed those areas heavily. The Ottoman troops also periodically invaded distant villages, where they slaughtered the residents in order to plunder their crops and livestock. At the same time, the Ottomans neglected the agricultural economy, which resulted in continuing economic decline. Because of these tactics, the Ottomans were viewed as oppressors by a hostile and uncooperative Libyan populace.

By the nineteenth century, the Ottoman Empire was in serious trouble throughout the region. Disagreements among the leadership and other factors made it increasingly difficult for the Ottomans to maintain control in their conquered lands. The Ottoman Empire became widely known as the "sick man of Europe." Libya was just one of its many languishing, undeveloped provinces.

AN ITALIAN COLONY

Given the weakened state of the Ottoman Empire, Italy in the early 1900s became interested in Libya as a place where it could extend its colonial power and dominance the way other European nations such as France and Britain had already done in other parts of the world. Italy expanded its trade to all the main Libyan ports and opened Italian schools and businesses in Libya, hoping to spread Italian culture and peacefully gain control of the region. Eventually, Italy decided that it needed to take a more aggressive approach. Judging correctly that other European powers would not stop them, the Italians in 1911 declared war on the Ottomans on the pretense that they had committed a hostile act against Italian commercial interests by arming Arab tribesmen in Libya.

Italy then invaded Libya on October 3, 1911, easily capturing Tripoli, Benghazi, and several other Libyan cities. By 1912 the Italian assault in Libya, coupled with other problems

LIBYAN POETRY

Poetry is one of Libya's longest traditions. One of Libya's most well-known poems was written by Sheikh Rajib Buhwaish Al-manfi. It describes the suffering and despair felt by thousands of Libyans who were forced into concentration camps set up by Italy between 1929 and 1931. Following are excerpts of the poem, taken from an English translation found on the Libyana Web site:

My only illness is being at al-Agailla camp, the imprisonment of my tribe and the long way from home . . .

My only illness is the loss of my beloved, good-looking strong people on top of camels and the best-looking horses . . .

My only illness is having to lose my dignity at my advanced age and the loss of our finest people, the ones we cannot do without . . .

My only illness is the torturing of our young women, with their bodies exposed . . .

My only illness is the loss of sweet and good people and having to be ruled by grotesque people whose straight faces show nothing but misery . . .

My only illness is the broken hearts, the falling tears and all the herds with no protector or care-taker . . .

THE LIBYAN RESISTANCE MOVEMENT

The Libyan resistance to Italian rule was led largely by a Muslim religious group called the Sanusi. Founded in the Arabian Peninsula in 1837 by Muhammad ibn Ali al-Sanusi (known as the "Grand Sanusi"), the group's goal was to strengthen Islam in the Arab world. The Sanusi fought in other areas as well, but the Italian invasion of Libya in 1911 led them to concentrate their interests there. The Sanusi moved their headquarters to Cyrenaica, where they built a large network of schools, hospitals, and community centers. The Sanusi also formed a strong political organization in Cyrenaica that rallied Libyans against the Italians for almost two decades. After Italian dictator Benito Mussolini destroyed Sanusi religious and educational centers in a brutal attack on Cyrenaica in 1922, however, the Sanusi movement was fatally weakened. Eventually, its leader, Idris al-Sanusi, was chosen to become the first ruler of Libya following its independence in 1951, but by then, Sanusi influence among the population was not very strong. King Idris was overthrown by Qaddafi revolutionaries in 1969. Qaddafi placed restrictions on Sanusi religious leaders and virtually banned the Sanusi movement.

within the empire, convinced the Ottomans to sign a peace treaty with Italy. The treaty called for the withdrawal of Ottoman troops, allowing Italy to formally declare both Tripolitania and Cyrenaica to be part of Italy. Italy then set about trying to pacify its newly won territories, a process that proved difficult because of Libyan resistance.

For Arabs, the Ottomans' surrender posed a threat to Islam, since the Italians, unlike the Ottomans, were not Muslims and were considered infidels, or nonbelievers. Although Italian troops managed to maintain control of Tripolitania, they encountered fierce resistance among the desert tribes in Fezzan and from a religious organization in Cyrenaica, a group called the Sanusi founded by Muhammad ibn Ali al-Sanusi in 1837. As a result, the Italian presence in Libya was largely confined to its coastal garrisons in Tripolitania.

In 1915 Italy agreed to enter World War I on the side of the Allies, a move that severely weakened Italy's grip on Libya. The demands of the war, as well as political and economic problems at home, forced Italy to reach compromises with the Libyan resisters. In 1917, for example, Italy signed a peace agreement with the leader of the Sanusi, Idris al-Sanusi, recognizing him as the emir of Cyrenaica. In addition, after a rebel government gained prominence in

Tripolitania, Italy granted that area greater self-government. By 1922 Tripolitania recognized Idris as emir of all of Libya, posing an undeniable threat to Italian rule over the area.

Fascist dictator Benito Mussolini's rise to power in Italy in 1922, however, renewed Italy's determination to subdue Libya. Under Mussolini's lead, Italy embarked on a reconquest of Libya—a land declared to be Italy's "fourth shore." As Mussolini himself explained, "Civilization . . . is what Italy is creating on the fourth shore of our sea."[4] Italy thus sent fresh troops to Libya in late 1922 to pacify the area by any means possible, a decision that began a decade of war in Libya. Libyans suffered greatly during this onslaught. Simons recounts, "The Libyan authorities have stated that some 750,000 people were killed during the Italian conquest, and . . . there is no doubt that many Libyan communities were displaced, slaughtered and driven into concentration camps."[5] The Italian attack on Cyrenaica in 1930 was particularly brutal. During the campaign, the Italians reportedly bombed

Italian immigrants in the 1930s travel to their new homes in Libya carting furniture given to them by the Italian government.

civilians, raped women, threw live prisoners from airplanes, and ran over others with tanks. Few Libyans escaped without loss and bloodshed. In January 1931, Italy announced that it had regained control of its fourth shore. The Italians divided Tripolitania and Cyrenaica into four provinces and called the entire area Libya.

Following Italy's victory, Italian immigrants poured into Libya. By 1940, 110,000 Italians had settled there, forming 12 percent of Libya's total population. With this infusion of Italian business expertise and funding, Libya made impressive economic progress. Agriculture was developed once again; public services were expanded; and roads, irrigation systems, and port facilities were improved. These improvements, however, were enjoyed mainly by the Italian settlers and a few loyal, high-ranking Arabs. The majority of Libyans received no education, jobs, or benefits, and many were uprooted when their land was given to Italians.

LIBYAN INDEPENDENCE

World War II marked the beginning of the end of Italian control over Libya. When Italy entered the war in 1940 on the side of Germany, Libyans contacted the British to offer sup-

In 1941 Australian soldiers charge the town of Bardia as part of the Allied offensive to drive the Italians from Libya.

KING IDRIS

King Idris al-Sanusi ruled Libya from 1951 until 1969, when he was overthrown by Muammar Qaddafi's revolutionary coup. Born in 1890, King Idris was the grandson of Muhammad ibn Ali al-Sanusi, the founder of the Sanusi religious movement in the mid-1800s. Idris was asked to become the group's leader in 1917. In 1920 he was acknowledged by Libya's Italian rulers as emir of Cyrenaica, but two years later he was forced to flee to Egypt when Italy attacked Sanusi forces in the region. Emir Idris returned to Libya after the end of World War II and spent several years trying to negotiate for Libya's independence. Finally, at the age of sixty-one, he became the king of Libya on December 24, 1951. The king, however, proved to be a weak leader; he had little support outside of Cyrenaica, was criticized for maintaining a close relationship with Britain and the United States, and failed to produce a male heir who could succeed him. After being overthrown by Qaddafi's forces in 1969, he lived in exile in Egypt until his death on May 25, 1983.

King Idris lacked broad support as Libya's monarch and proved to be an unpopular leader.

port to the Allies against Italy. The Libyans also rallied once again behind resistance leader Idris al-Sanusi and at a meeting in Cairo, Egypt, in August 1940 gave him the authority to cooperate with Britain for Libyan independence.

The war itself subjected Libya to yet another round of devastation and destruction, because North Africa became one of the major battle theaters of World War II. Thousands of Libyan Arabs were killed, and the country's economy was once again shattered as the Allied armies of Britain, France, and the United States battled Italian and German forces in the region. During the ferocious battles, however, the British managed to gain control of both Cyrenaica and Tripolitania, and by February 1943 Italian and German forces were driven out of Libya. Britain and France governed Libya as caretakers for the balance of the war.

With Germany's and Italy's defeat at the end of World War II, Libya was finally freed. During the 1945 Potsdam Conference, the Allies agreed to terminate Italy's right to the area. Although some nations wanted a UN trusteeship to be set up in Libya, with independence to come later, Britain proposed that Libya be granted immediate independence. In 1949, with Britain's support, Idris al-Sanusi unilaterally declared Cyrenaica an independent emirate. In November of that year, the UN passed a resolution calling for the creation of a Libyan sovereign state no later than January 1, 1952. A group of twenty-one Libyans named by the UN set up the National Constituent Assembly. This body convened for the first time in November 1950 and approved a federation system of government with three provinces—Cyrenaica, Tripolitania, and Fezzan—under a monarchy, or king. A constitution was approved in October 1951. On December 24, 1951, King Idris I proudly proclaimed Libya's independence as the United Kingdom of Libya.

OIL DISCOVERIES

Despite its newly independent and united status, Libya remained divided. Its federation government was weak, and the king had broad powers over the legislature that he frequently abused. In fact, after the very first elections in 1952, the king abolished political parties to suppress criticism of his rule. In addition, partly because King Idris came from Cyrenaica and might favor that area, there were frictions between the two provinces of Tripolitania and Cyrenaica concerning the amount of power held by the federal government. An effort was made to ease these tensions by alternating the capital of Libya between Tripoli and Benghazi, but provincial disputes continued.

Libya also continued to be an extremely poor and illiterate country. As American economist John Lindberg commented at the time, "The standard of living is extremely low; a large part of the population lives in caves, lacking furniture and the simplest conveniences. Clothing is made out of home grown wool. The poor are clad in rags and walk barefoot, even during the fairly cold winters."[6] To help ease such problems, Libya relied on foreign aid, particularly from Great

Britain. In 1953, in exchange for allowing Britain to establish military bases in Libya, the two nations signed a twenty-year agreement of friendship that committed the British to providing economic aid to Libya. Libya also signed an agreement with the United States, which paid to establish a U.S. military base near Tripoli (the Wheelus Air Force Base). These agreements, along with UN development aid, helped Libya survive during its early years as a sovereign nation.

In 1959, however, Libya's fortunes suddenly changed when major oil reserves were discovered in Cyrenaica by the U.S. oil company Esso (later renamed Exxon). Discoveries of additional reserves followed, and Libya's high-quality oil was quickly developed for commercial export to Europe. The flow of income from the production of crude oil soon changed Libya from a struggling, impoverished country into a wealthy nation. As the decade of the 1960s began, it was clear that Libya's discovery of oil riches marked a turning point in its history.

3

Qaddafi's Libya

The fragile Libyan monarchy that took power after Libya's independence in 1951 did not last long enough to lead the country into its prosperous future. Instead, Libya's journey as an oil-producing nation has been led by Muammar Qaddafi, a revolutionary leader who used Libya's oil wealth to produce greater prosperity for Libyans but also earned Libya an international reputation as a nation that supports terrorism.

A Libyan Revolution

In the 1960s, Libya's monarchy was seen as weak and repressive by many Libyans because of the government's tendencies to tightly hold power and suppress dissent. Corruption in government construction contracts, the government's failure to use oil wealth to benefit the larger population, and King Idris's alliances with Western countries such as Britain and the United States created an even higher level of hostility toward the monarchy among the Libyan people.

After years of foreign domination, repression, and poverty, many Libyans simply became disenchanted with King Idris's failure to use the country's new oil wealth to forge a responsive Libyan government or improve the standard of living. Instead, the government's policies largely enriched an elite group of wealthy merchants by granting them lucrative government contracts and selling them agricultural land. This favoritism left working-class Libyans at the mercy of the wealthy. The poor flocked to congested and overcrowded

Muammar Qaddafi was a young army officer at the time of his participation in the 1969 coup that toppled Libya's monarchy.

MUAMMAR QADDAFI

Muammar Qaddafi, a charismatic, complex, and proud leader, has ruled Libya since he and his followers staged a military coup in 1969 to overthrow Libya's aging King Idris. Qaddafi was born in a Bedouin tent in 1942, during World War II. His parents were poor, supported by farming and a small herd of goats and camels. As a youngster, Qaddafi listened to his father's stories about the Italian occupation of Libya and Libyan resistance. When he was about seven years old, his family hired a religious tutor. Later, he attended elementary and secondary school but, because of his poverty and Bedouin background, he was treated like an outcast. During Qaddafi's teenage years, he witnessed a movement in the Arab world toward greater Arab pride, unity, and independence. The movement was led by Egypt's President Gamal Abdel Nasser.

All of these experiences contributed to Qaddafi's character: He grew up to be a devoutly religious man, proud of his Bedouin roots, concerned about Libya's poor, and devoted to Arab causes and Libyan independence. In 1963 Qaddafi attended the Military Academy in Benghazi and became an army officer, graduating in 1965. While at the academy, he and a group of fellow officers formed a secret committee that plotted the overthrow of King Idris. In 1969 these plans were finally put into action, and Qaddafi led a successful coup against the government and became Libya's new leader. Since then, despite reported dissatisfaction with his rule and an international record of supporting terrorism, Qaddafi has maintained a tight hold on power. He remains Libya's leader today.

Qaddafi has always been proud of his Bedouin roots. Here, he poses with members of his family in his father's tent.

shantytowns around Benghazi and Tripoli to fight for what jobs and wages were available. Furthermore, when some of Libya's low-paid workers in various industries began to organize into trade unions to bargain for higher pay and better working conditions, the government thwarted the union effort by arresting union leaders, replacing striking workers, and enacting repressive labor laws.

Another development that undercut support for King Idris was the rise of an Egyptian leader, Gamal Abdel Nasser. Nasser advocated Pan-Arabism, a pro-Arab, anti-Western political philosophy that sought to unite Arab countries to increase their political and military power and boost Arab pride. Nasser's brand of Arab nationalism appealed to Libya's Arabs, particularly the younger generation, many of whom saw Libya's close ties with Western nations as a threat to Arab independence. As a result of this anti-Western sentiment, Libyans pressured the king in 1964 to ask both the British and the Americans to evacuate their Libyan military bases before the dates agreed to in their treaties. Britain withdrew most of its forces by 1966, and the U.S. base was closed in 1970.

Rising discontent and agitation against Libya's government soon led to revolution. On September 1, 1969, King Idris was toppled by a revolutionary coup staged by a group of army officers (the Free Officers Movement) led by a young and charismatic military colonel named Muammar Qaddafi. Qaddafi had been critical of the government for more than ten years and was a strong supporter of Nasser's philosophy of Arab nationalism. Within a few hours, Qaddafi's group secured key government offices, radio stations, airports, and police stations in Tripoli, Benghazi, and other cities. The coup was a peaceful one. King Idris was out of the country at the time for medical treatment. Libya's army units rallied to support the coup, and the Libyan people enthusiastically embraced the new government.

Just after dawn on September 1, Qaddafi broadcast the new government's first message to the Libyan people:

> People of Libya. In response to your own will, fulfilling your most heartfelt wishes, . . . your armed forces have undertaken the overthrow of the reactionary and corrupt regime, the stench of which has sickened and horrified us all. At a single blow your gallant army has toppled

these idols and has destroyed their images. By a single stroke it has lightened the long dark night in which the Turkish domination was followed first by Italian rule, then by this reactionary and decadent regime, which was no more than a hotbed of extortion, faction, treachery and treason.[7]

In the radio speech, Qaddafi also explained that Libya would be a republic and promised to provide opportunity for all:

> From this day forward, Libya is a free, self-governing republic. She will adopt the name of The Libyan Arab Republic and will, by the grace of God, begin her task. She will advance on the road to freedom, the path of unity and social justice, guaranteeing to all her citizens and throwing wide in front of them the gate of honest employment, where injustice and exploitation are banished, where no-one will count himself master and servant, and where all will be free, brothers in a society in which, with God's help, prosperity and equality will be seen to rule us all.[8]

Within a few days, it became clear that the Revolutionary Command Council (RCC), a twelve-member group of officers from the Free Officers Movement, was in charge of the country. Qaddafi was named commander in chief of the armed forces and became the new head of state.

THE QADDAFI GOVERNMENT

For Qaddafi, the coup was a true revolution, and he set about forming a new type of government—one that would purge the country of all vestiges of foreign influences, emphasize Arab unity, and provide sweeping, socialist economic reforms to benefit ordinary Libyans. Soon after the coup, therefore, the government expelled Italians and a few Jews still living in Libya and took over their property. It canceled treaties with Britain and the United States and replaced Western street names and signs with Arabic ones. The government also implemented immediate economic measures, including rent reductions, doubling of the minimum wage, and a government takeover of foreign banks.

Qaddafi, however, made clear that only his ideas would be implemented. The government created a political party

QADDAFI'S *GREEN BOOK*

Qaddafi outlined his revolutionary theories in a three-volume book called *The Green Book*. Written in a clear, readable style with numerous political slogans, the book contains three parts addressing political organization, the economy, and social issues, published respectively in 1974, 1977, and 1978. In part 1 of the book (called "The Solution of the Problem of Democracy"), Qaddafi announces his view that most democracies employ undemocratic systems in which people's interests are represented by others. He argues for a system of "direct democracy" in which everyone participates in debating and deciding political issues. In part 2 of *The Green Book* ("The Solution of the Economic Problem: 'Socialism'"), Qaddafi discusses the relationship between workers and employers and concludes that, to be free, workers must be partners instead of employees and must be able to meet human needs such as having a house, a vehicle, and enough income to live a comfortable life. In part 3 ("The Social Basis of the Third Universal Theory"), Qaddafi spells out his views on matters such as religion, education, and the role of women. For example, he says that a nation should have one religion (Islam in Libya) and that men and women should have equal rights to education and to pursue their "natural" roles. Many ideas from *The Green Book* became public policy in Libya over the years of Qaddafi's rule. Today, however, its influence is dwindling. In fact, Libya has changed many of Qaddafi's socialist policies in an effort to improve its struggling economy.

called the Arab Socialist Union (ASU) but prohibited the formation of other political parties. Unions were banned, along with other organizations and associations, and citizens were advised not to express views contrary to those of the leadership. The press was censored and used as a tool of propaganda to support the revolutionary government; only the regime's newspaper was funded, and radio and television were required to promote the revolution. Most Libyans, especially the poor, did not oppose these measures, hoping the new government would provide them with a better life.

Despite these restrictions, Qaddafi called his government a new form of direct democracy, part of a cultural revolution that he formally announced in April 1973 and later developed into a three-part book called *The Green Book*. In this book, Qaddafi's plan, the "Third Universal Theory," emphasizes the importance of the people in decision making and administration but rejects political parties or the election of representatives—the hallmarks of representative democracy as practiced in America and other democratic countries. Instead, under Qaddafi's plan, local political bodies, called "people's committees," were created to allow Libyans to directly convey their interests to the government. By the end of 1973, over two thousand of these people's committees were established throughout Libya. Another part of Qaddafi's vision for government was the General People's Congress (GPC), a national body made up of citizens. The GPC was the organ charged with governing the country.

The new political vision was fully manifested in March 1977, when the GPC renamed Libya the Socialist People's Libyan Arab Jamahiriya, a name that means "state of the masses" and refers to Qaddafi's idea that people should govern themselves without representation. The GPC also named Qaddafi its general secretary and created the General Secretariat, composed of RCC members, and the General People's Committee, a body made up of various secretaries (or ministers), to carry out the day-to-day running of the country. Under this system, all citizens had the right and duty to participate in their local people's congresses, and their decisions were to be passed up to the GPC for implementation by the General Secretariat and the General People's Committee. With this reorganization of government, Qaddafi achieved what he called "people's power."

Nevertheless, Qaddafi continued to tinker with the structure of Libya's government, introducing a new concept of revolutionary committees in 1977. These committees were created to "guide" the people's committees, essentially to ensure the people's allegiance to the Qaddafi regime and prevent opposition to the government's programs. In 1979 Qaddafi again reorganized the government; at this point he resigned as secretary of the GPC and became simply "leader of the revolution."

Qaddafi's political system did provide for some debate and consultation at local levels on local and domestic concerns, but it was difficult for people's congresses to discuss matters of foreign policy, defense, or oil. These types of issues often arose too quickly to be put before the local people and frequently required a great deal of expertise and information before decisions could be made. Also, many Libyans either lacked the necessary education and understanding or simply did not want to become involved in political issues. Women especially, despite encouragement, often were not interested in politics. Inevitably, therefore, Qaddafi's system of direct democracy became a representative system in which local leaders represented the people's interests.

Moreover, the growth of revolutionary committees in later years placed the entire process under the watchful, controlling eye of Qaddafi's government, contradicting the very principles of freedom and democracy. As Simons explains, "The revolutionary committees came to serve as one of the main bulwarks for the security of the [Qaddafi] regime."[9] With this development, the local people's congresses ceased being free, decision-making bodies and became simply a tool to communicate the government's decisions to the people and a way to keep Libyans from challenging the revolution's ideas. Although Qaddafi describes his country as a government run by the people, as Professor Dirk Vandewalle notes, "In reality, Libya remains a political system where its leader and a few close advisors make virtually all decisions."[10]

QADDAFI'S ECONOMIC PROGRAMS

Qaddafi sought to gain support for the revolution by increasing oil production and distributing Libya's oil revenues to benefit all parts of Libya's population. The government vastly improved health care and education and provided many new social welfare benefits. Qaddafi also built new housing, provided interest-free home loans, and banned rental payments for property, eliminating the private real estate market and making renters instant property owners. To further equalize wealth in Libya, the government made changes in the currency system and froze bank deposits of wealthier Libyans.

In addition, although the government initially encouraged some private businesses, it eventually nationalized, or took control of, most companies and created a number of new state-owned corporations. By the late 1970s the government controlled the oil industry and the country's infrastructure (roads, communications, ports, airports, and electricity). It also had become the only importer and provider of all important products, including automobiles, livestock, construction materials, fertilizers, and services such as insurance, banking, advertising, and publishing. The government mandated that workers share in the profits of these businesses; often, a worker's share of the profits exceeded his salary, lifting many desperately poor Libyans to middle-class status. In 1978, employing the slogan "partners not wage earners,"[11]Qaddafi went a step further, urging workers to take over management of their companies.

Soon, small retail trading businesses, such as the many privately run small shops and traditional markets (called *souks*), were put out of business. To replace these markets, the government set up hundreds of large centralized stores. These state-owned supermarkets, as *Los Angeles Times* reporter Mariam Sami describes, "sold everything from imported shampoos to washing machines, and even cars, at subsidized prices."[12] By 1981 Qaddafi had virtually eliminated all private enterprise and made the government the sole provider of goods.

Qaddafi's efforts largely eliminated poverty, provided good jobs, and greatly improved the lives of poorer Libyans. Benefits reached even to the oasis towns in the inland deserts, and were received by the people with great appreciation,

Qaddafi announces his plan to nationalize Libya's oil industry. By the late 1970s, the Libyan government assumed complete control of the country's oil companies.

making Qaddafi a very popular leader among much of the Libyan populace in the early days of the revolution. Yet these policies had long-term costs. They created a bureaucratic nightmare for the government, which was supposed to distribute the funds and manage the various programs. They often resulted in inefficient, poorly managed businesses that were more of an economic drain than a contribution. The policies bankrupted and alienated wealthier Libyans, causing many educated and experienced citizens to leave the country. At the same time, by providing so many free or easy benefits, the programs created a native workforce that was not inclined to work hard or learn new skills. Another result was a dependence on a large number of foreign workers to man the technical jobs. Overall, Qaddafi's policies resulted in a stalled economy that ultimately failed to provide many needed goods and services.

By focusing on distribution of wealth to the people rather than on development of industry, therefore, most observers believe that Libya neglected to build a firm foundation for the future growth of its economy.

QADDAFI AND THE ARAB WORLD

Although Qaddafi made economic changes that helped give him popular appeal within his own country, he pursued a foreign policy that alienated Libya in the international world. Qaddafi's goal was to promote Arab unity and fight Western imperialism. One of Qaddafi's greatest ambitions was to see a free and independent Palestinian state. He therefore backed the Palestinian people's fight against the Israelis, who with Western support had built their nation upon lands claimed by Palestinians. Most of Qaddafi's support took the form of funding sent to the Al-Fatah organization, a group, led by Yasir Arafat, that used guerrilla military techniques (such as hit-and-run attacks and bombings) to strike at Israeli targets.

Qaddafi also tried to join forces with Egypt and other Arab nations to promote the Palestinian struggle and other Arab causes. In 1970 he was able to form an Arab federation between Libya, Egypt, Sudan, and Syria—the Federation of Arab Republics—to cooperate on economic, political, and military issues. The federation, however, failed as a result of nonparticipation by Sudan and Egypt's fears that Qaddafi was too hot-headed and immature as a leader.

Libya's relations with Egypt soured when Qaddafi, in retaliation for Israel's shooting of a Libyan passenger airplane in Israeli territory in 1973, ordered an Egyptian submarine based in Tripoli to torpedo a British ocean liner carrying American Jews. Egypt's President Anwar Sadat quickly countermanded the order. Egypt also left Qaddafi out of its plans for a 1973 war against Israel, a clear snub because Qaddafi sought to portray himself as the leader among Arabs on the issue of Palestine. As a result of these types of disagreements with other Arab leaders, Qaddafi's Libya soon became isolated within the Arab world.

Qaddafi (seated, second from left) was an early supporter of Yasir Arafat (seated, third from left), who used terrorist tactics to challenge the Israeli government.

LIBYA AND INTERNATIONAL TERRORISM

Disillusioned with more moderate Arab views, Qaddafi began supporting radical Palestinian organizations, such as Black September, a group that specialized in the use of international terrorism to achieve its goals. This group became notorious for killing eleven Israelis at the Munich Olympic Games in September 1972. Following this attack, in a gesture that clearly indicated Libya's support, Qaddafi flew the bodies of five of the slain Black September terrorists to Libya for ceremonial funerals.

Over the next two decades, Qaddafi also helped finance, arm, and train foreign insurgents fighting for various other radical causes. For example, Qaddafi was linked to radical European groups such as the Irish Republican Army in Northern Ireland, the Red Army Faction in Germany, and the

Basque Separatist Movement in Spain. In addition, Qaddafi gave substantial financial support to the Sandinistas, a leftist government in Nicaragua that was battling U.S.-backed opposition forces. In 1980 Qaddafi sent Libyan troops into the neighboring country of Chad to support one side in that country's civil war. Indeed, according to Israeli intelligence reports, by 1986 Qaddafi was supporting about fifty insurgent groups as well as numerous radical governments.

Qaddafi defended his foreign aid policies as part of Libya's commitment to "liberation movements"[13] similar to the one that had brought him to power. Many of the groups supported by Libya, however, were considered to be terrorists by the United States and other Western countries, and by the 1980s Libya was widely viewed as a terrorist country. For this reason, the relationship between Libya and the United States became very strained. Libyan policies caused the United States in 1978 to ban the export of U.S. military and nuclear

QADDAFI'S MILITARY

Libya, under Qaddafi, became a highly militarized nation. Qaddafi and his followers rapidly expanded the Libyan armed forces after the 1969 coup, and one of the priorities of Qaddafi's revolutionary government was to build up Libya's armaments as quickly as possible. This buildup began with purchases such as jet aircraft and armored vehicles and grew over the years to include stockpiling of chemical and biological weapons as well as a program to develop nuclear weapons. Initially, Qaddafi acquired items such as aircraft from France, but later, after the Western nations became reluctant to provide him with weapons, Qaddafi turned to the Soviet Union to purchase arms. Throughout the 1970s and 1980s, Libya became one of the world's largest arms importers, obtaining many weapons from the Soviets. Libya also at times loaned its armaments to others, such as when its aircraft were flown by Egyptians during the 1973 war with Israel.

By 2002 Libya's armed forces were estimated at seventy-six thousand soldiers. In December 2003, however, as part of an effort to improve its international relations, Libya announced that it would halt its unconventional weapons programs, eliminate its stockpiles of chemical and biological weapons, and submit to international verification and supervision. Since then, inspectors have searched Libya to locate weapons stockpiles and equipment related to its nuclear program. In January 2004, Libya allowed the United States to airlift fifty-five thousand pounds of documents and weapons components out of Libya.

equipment to the country. Later in 1981, U.S. president Ronald Reagan launched a broader campaign against Libyan terrorism. As part of the strategy, the United States pressured Libya by scheduling military maneuvers off the Libyan coast, an action that led to military confrontation when the United States shot down two Libyan jet fighters sent to monitor the American activities. In 1982, at a time when the United States was buying about a third of Libya's oil, President Reagan ordered a ban on all Libyan oil imports. In 1986, suspecting that Libya was involved in various international terrorist attacks against Americans, the United States bombed Libya, striking airfields, antiaircraft sites, and a compound housing Qaddafi and his family. The strikes killed as many as one hundred Libyans, including Qaddafi's infant daughter. That same year, the United States imposed comprehensive economic sanctions to prevent American companies from doing business with Libya. The U.S. government also froze some $200 million in Libyan assets in the United States. These and other efforts to weaken and topple Qaddafi made the Libyan leader increasingly isolated by the late 1980s.

Residents of Tripoli survey damage after a 1986 U.S. air strike. The United States bombed Libya in retaliation for Qaddafi's involvement in terrorist operations.

In 1988 investigators search the fuselage of Pan Am Flight 103 in Lockerbie, Scotland. Two Libyans were charged with planting the bomb that downed the airliner.

THE LOCKERBIE BOMBING

The difficult relationship between Libya and the United States worsened when U.S. officials charged Libya with responsibility for the bombing of an American aircraft, Pan Am Flight 103, over Lockerbie, Scotland, in 1988. This terrorist incident claimed the lives of 259 passengers, along with 11 of the town's residents. It was the most lethal terrorist act until the September 11, 2001, attack on the World Trade Center. Libya was not immediately suspected, but in 1991 U.S. and British investigators found evidence linking two Libyan intelligence agents, Abdelbaset Al-Megrahi and Al Amin Khalifa Fhimah, to the crime. They were charged in both British and American courts of planting a bomb on board the aircraft. Libya denied the accusation, claiming it had no knowledge of the incident.

The UN Security Council demanded that Libya surrender the two agents for trial, disclose everything it knew about the crime, and pay compensation—in essence, admit responsibility even before trial. In response, Libya offered to conduct its own investigation and cooperate with the UN, but this gesture was rejected by U.S. and British officials. Instead, in 1992 the two countries persuaded the UN to adopt a resolution imposing economic sanctions on Libya that prohibited most flights to or from Libya, banned military dealings with Libya, and urged UN members to reduce their staff at Libyan diplomatic missions. Additional sanctions were imposed in 1993 to freeze Libyan assets in foreign countries and prohibit most foreign business activities in Libya.

The sanctions severely damaged the Libyan economy and led to years of recriminations between Libya and the international community. The Libyan government charged that the matter should have been dealt with in the International Court of Justice (ICJ), a judicial body that decides disputes between countries. This demand was met in 1998 when the ICJ agreed to hear Libya's case. This ruling for Libya led to a compromise within the UN Security Council: a trial of the two suspects held in a neutral country, the Netherlands.

Ultimately, however, the Lockerbie incident forced Libya to curb its radical foreign policy behaviors. The Libyan government presented a careful, reasonable response in order to improve Libya's image in the international community and gain the support of the ICJ and the UN. Journalist Khalil I. Matar and attorney Robert W. Thabit explain: "[Qaddafi] managed the Lockerbie crisis in a way that transformed the role of most international organizations into one that defended or supported Libya's positions."[14] Libya also responded to the UN demands for turning over information, paid compensation to some victims, and asked terrorists remaining in Libya to leave the country. By 1999 even the U.S. State Department acknowledged that Libya no longer seemed to be involved in terrorism.

Finally, after mediation by Saudi crown prince Bandar and African leader Nelson Mandela, Libya on March 15, 1999, agreed to turn over the suspected Libyan terrorists to the UN for trial for the Lockerbie incident. One of the two, Al-Megrahi, was found guilty in 2001 and sentenced to life imprisonment. The other was acquitted for insufficient evidence. Later, negotiations resolved the remaining issue of compensation to victims, paving the way for the lifting of UN sanctions in 2003. As the new millennium dawned, Libya was ruled by a more subdued Qaddafi, his revolutionary fervor seemingly reduced by both economic and political disappointments.

4

A TRADITIONAL LAND

For centuries, religion, tradition, and tribal values have dominated the lives of people inhabiting the area now called Libya. Qaddafi's government, however, sought to eliminate tribal and religious leaders and weaken family and tribal ties. Yet despite Qaddafi's efforts at reform, Libya continues to be a highly traditional land.

ISLAM AND TRADITION IN LIBYA

The family is the core of Libya's tribal system. Historically, family traditions and values formed the basis for Libyans' social and political life, and family leaders were the source of all authority. As Library of Congress writer LaVerle Berry explains, "The family [in Libya] was the most important focus of attention and loyalty and source of security, followed by the tribe. In most cases, the most powerful family of a clan provided tribal leadership and determined the reputation and power of the tribe."[15] Religion also was a strong part of tribal life, and prominent family and tribal leaders were usually the recognized religious leaders as well.

After Libya's independence, under the rule of King Idris, the government relied on traditional tribal and religious leaders to carry out its business at local levels. These leaders were given the power to grant appointments to government positions and hand out government contracts. They enriched merchants and placed many loyal tribesmen into positions as administrators, hospital directors, and oil industry officials. This practice created a privileged class within Libyan society that enjoyed most of the benefits of Libya's oil wealth during the 1950s and 1960s.

Tribal and religious rule therefore remained strong in prerevolutionary Libya. People looked to local tribal and religious leaders as the true authorities, and despite the differences between rich and poor, most Libyans took great pride in their tribal membership and values.

TRIPOLI'S OLD CITY

As part of its efforts to promote traditional culture, Libya has restored many traditional buildings located in the part of Tripoli known as the old city, or the medina. This area is an ancient walled city dating from Roman times with narrow streets and alleyways and buildings that shade pedestrians from the sun. The street side of homes in the medina are simple and unadorned, to maintain privacy and prevent curiosity, but interior doors, windows, and courtyards have archways and decorative detailing made from tile, wood, and plasterwork. The medina also is home to seven mosques, each featuring elaborate architectural work. Following Libya's independence in 1951, many traditional families from the medina moved out of the area to live in newer, more modern houses abandoned by departing Italians. As a result of this migration, many older homes and mosques were left empty and fell into disrepair. In the 1970s, however, the government of Libya restored many of these buildings to their former glory, and the medina is once again considered a jewel of traditional Libyan architecture.

Pictured are the ornately decorated minarets of a mosque in Tripoli's medina. In recent decades, the Libyan government has restored many of Tripoli's old buildings.

QADDAFI AND ISLAM

When Qaddafi came to power, he relied on religion as a way to achieve legitimacy for his new government. Qaddafi referred to the importance of Islam in his very first communication, stating, "[The Revolutionary Command Council] believes profoundly in the freedom of religion and in the moral values contained in the Qur'an [Islam's holy book], and it promises to defend these and uphold these."[16] True to his word, Qaddafi, a devout Muslim, implemented religious reforms to reaffirm fundamental Islamic values and make Islam the center of Libyans' lives. The government, for example, enacted laws to prohibit the use of alcoholic beverages, outlaw prostitution, and ban nightclubs. The government also turned churches into mosques and readopted a revised Islamic calendar. In 1970 the RCC eliminated the monarchy's system of dual civil and religious courts in which religion was used only for personal status matters (such as marriage, divorce, and child custody), and instead required all laws to conform to sharia, or religious law. Among the laws adopted were religious penalties, such as one that punished armed robbery by amputation of a hand and a foot. Other laws called for flogging of individuals who fail to observe Ramadan, an Islamic holiday, and for eighty lashes to be administered to both men and women guilty of having sex outside of marriage. Qaddafi himself gave religious as well as political advice and appeared to see himself as a pious Muslim called by God to interpret Islam for the Libyan people.

Qaddafi leads a group of students in prayer in Tripoli in 1973. Qaddafi views himself as a pious Muslim sent by God to lead the Libyan people.

Qaddafi's revolutionary plan later emphasized Islam as the basis for his political beliefs. As historian John Wright explains, according to Qaddafi, "Islam had set out the guiding principles for economic management, labour relations,

prosperity, justice and free society."[17] Qaddafi believed that Islamic principles required a moral society that was neither capitalist nor communist but in which the rich would not be allowed to oppress or exploit the poor.

Despite Qaddafi's support for religion, however, he deliberately sought to reduce the power of traditional religious and tribal leaders, whom he feared might threaten the revolution. The committee charged with revising the legal code to conform to sharia, for example, contained only two people familiar with religious law. In addition, the Qaddafi system used the *qadis*, or religious judges, who traditionally applied sharia in deciding personal status cases, only as consultants. Though Qaddafi accepted the sharia, he was less willing to accept the interpretations of religious law by religious leaders; instead, he believed that each individual could interpret Islamic law for himself. In the end, therefore, the changes Qaddafi made to Libya's laws by the imposition of sharia were limited.

In yet another effort to end the power of traditional leaders, Qaddafi eliminated *waqf*, a system in which property owned by Islamic groups was excluded from taxation and inheritance law. This abolished the main income source for religious leaders, bringing them under Qaddafi's control. Emboldened, Qaddafi in 1973 proclaimed an Islamic revolution, using the occasion to publicly reject as error various bodies of religious law that had been developed by religious scholars and judges over many centuries. In 1975 Qaddafi issued a decree that ordered religious leaders not to comment on political issues.

Qaddafi has rejected all criticism of his policies, maintaining that his is a populist form of Islam and that the revolution, not religious leadership, is the true embodiment of Islamic teachings. Many believe, however, that Qaddafi has simply used Islam to gain support for his policies. According to political analyst George Joffe, "Islam in Libya is one more instrument of popular sovereignty—but an instrument closely controlled and supervised . . . by the regime itself."[18]

QADDAFI AND TRIBAL LOYALTIES
At the same time that Qaddafi was redefining Islam for Libyans, he also began attacking their tribal affiliations. Berry explains: "Despite his beduin roots, [Qaddafi] viewed

tribes as anachronistic and as obstacles to modernization."[19] The government, therefore, tried to break the links between people and their tribal roots. The regime, for example, encouraged all Libyans, not only tribal leaders, to become involved in political decision making as part of local people's committees. Other policies, such as Qaddafi's agricultural land reclamation scheme, encouraged Libyans to resettle and farm on reclaimed land that often was far away from their tribal homelands. Once there, villagers were provided with schools, hospitals, electricity, and other modern conveniences to convince them to stay.

In the cities, Qaddafi's government launched a campaign against the privileged classes who owed their positions and wealth to religious and tribal leaders, dismissing many from jobs in government agencies and government-owned businesses. A new system was then implemented for acquiring jobs in the new government, one that was based on education and revolutionary zeal rather than family or tribal status and loyalty. Later, the government passed laws restricting the amount of wealth and property people could accumulate, further limiting the power of the elite classes. These types of programs helped to diminish the influence of local tribal and religious leaders and to weaken Libyans' identification with their tribal heritage.

RESISTANCE TO QADDAFI'S POLICIES
Qaddafi's efforts to forge a national political identity in place of traditional tribal and religious relationships, however, have been met by resistance from many Libyans. Qaddafi's actions against religious laws and traditions, for example, angered religious leaders and scholars, who claimed that the reforms were contrary to Islam and that Qaddafi was simply using Islam to promote his revolution. Many spoke out against the regime, but some who did suddenly and mysteriously disappeared. Sheikh al-Bishti, an influential religious leader from Tripoli, for example, disappeared in 1980 after condemning Qaddafi's regime for many years. Various Islamist groups who opposed Qaddafi's rule met with similar fates. In 1987, for example, nine members of a Muslim group called Holy War were publicly executed by the government.

Many Libyans unhappy with Qaddafi's vision simply left the country. Some formed opposition groups in exile. One

FIVE PILLARS OF ISLAM

The religion of Islam was founded in A.D. 610 by the prophet Muhammad. Followers of Islam, called Muslims, believe in one God ("Allah" in Arabic) and follow the values contained in the Koran, the Islamic holy book. The most important religious duties in Islam are contained in what are called its "five pillars": (1) *shahada*, an affirmation of faith that must be recited daily ("There is no god but Allah, and Muhammad is his prophet"); (2) *salat*, prayer performed five times a day; (3) *zakat*, payment of a religious tax to benefit the poor; (4) *sawm*, daytime fasting (or refraining from eating, drinking, smoking, or having sex) during one month of the year (October) called Ramadan; and (5) hajj, a pilgrimage to Mecca, which is considered the birthplace of Islam.

Libyan men pray during one of the five prayer times Muslims observe each day.

of these, the National Front for the Salvation of Libya (NFSL), staged an unsuccessful coup attempt to overthrow Qaddafi in 1984. Another group, Al-Burkan, sought to assassinate Libyan officials associated with Qaddafi's government. To deal with this outside opposition, the government implemented a policy of hunting down and assassinating the Libyan exiles. Scholar Lillian Craig Harris states that between

1980 and 1986, "twenty anti-Qadhafi Libyans had been assassinated abroad."[20]

Much of the rest of Libyan society slowly became alienated from politics and the Qaddafi regime. Despite government efforts to encourage Libyans to participate in the people's congresses, many do not participate. They choose to remain passive in Qaddafi's revolution, either because of disinterest in Qaddafi's vision or fear that the government will persecute them if they say something critical of Qaddafi.

THE CONTINUING IMPORTANCE OF FAMILY

Most Libyans simply seek refuge in their families, their religious faith, and tradition. As Harris explains,

> Despite the lip service paid Qadhafi's . . . revolution, it was largely disregarded by the populace. Most Libyans remain reluctant to involve themselves in government affairs. . . . Their usual response to political pressures appears to be a deepened interest in the private affairs of the family and immediate circle—that is, a reinforcing of traditional values.[21]

Family connections therefore remain the core of Libyan society.

In fact, as Qaddafi's revolutionary zeal disrupted other social contacts such as business, professional, and social organizations, family and tribe became increasingly important, as virtually the only remaining source of social activities. As political science professor Lisa Anderson notes, "In the absence of alternatives, Libyans found themselves once again reliant upon kinship ties for much of their social intercourse, economic welfare and political identity."[22] This return to family and tribal ties can even be seen in the elections to the local people's committees, in which many leaders run and are elected based on their family and tribal connections. Even after Qaddafi's political reforms, the traditional system of family and tribal leadership has reemerged.

For many Libyan women especially, families are still the source of their identity and personal power. As Rahab Adhams, a female principal of a girls' school, explains, "The family is my empire."[23] This dedication to family can also be seen in the fact that many young Libyans who have been permitted to leave the country for education return to live in Libya. The basic unit of traditional Libyan life—the family—thus continues in many cases to outweigh all other interests and loyalties.

WOMEN AND TRADITION

One area in particular—women's rights—illustrates the people's reluctance to abandon tradition and embrace Qaddafi's reforms. Before the revolution, men were considered the head of families and women traditionally were secluded at home, their only role to take care of the home and the children. Women were expected to be modest and virtuous; they were to cover their bodies with a long robe and veil whenever they appeared in public, and their virginity before marriage was considered essential to the family's honor. Marriages were arranged by parents, and often young girls were married to much older men. The bride, after marriage, went to the home of the husband's family, where she lived under the watchful eye of her mother-in-law. Her only claim to status

Many women in Qaddafi's Libya continue to adhere to traditional Muslim practices. Here, Libyan women are wearing long robes that conceal their entire bodies.

A woman studies at a university established by Qaddafi as part of his larger effort to promote woman's rights.

was to become pregnant and produce a male heir. In addition, Islamic law gave men much greater freedom in marriages. They were permitted to have up to four wives and could divorce their wives with little difficulty (by simply stating "I divorce thee" three times before witnesses), whereas women could have only one husband and had limited ability to initiate divorce proceedings.

Unlike some areas of Islamic values that the government sought to reinforce, Qaddafi wanted to emancipate women from this traditional seclusion and repression. To do so, he urged women to become educated and to work, and he guaranteed them equal treatment under the law. Immediately after Qaddafi seized power the government passed laws affirming the equality of men and women and requiting equal pay for women working in the same occupations as men. Additional laws were passed regarding marriage and divorce; women were required to be sixteen years old to marry and they could marry without their parents' approval. Other laws gave social security protections to widows, female divorcées over age forty, and unmarried mothers. In addition, working women became entitled to maternity leave and other benefits. Qaddafi's policies also promoted educational opportunities for women, and they were urged to participate in political activities. In 1984 Libya required female students of secondary schools to participate in military training.

As a result of these revolutionary changes, Libyan women were given new opportunities for education, and all professions, including military service, became open to them. Despite these opportunities, however, Libyan society has been slow to change. Although many women took advantage of educational programs, for example, a significant number of rural women still do not attend school past the age required by the government. Many women also rejected Qaddafi's ideas about women in the workforce and instead continued to follow very traditional roles working as wives and mothers in the home. Men, meanwhile, continued to act as the heads of families and hold most influential positions in society. As LaVerle Berry notes, "female participation in the workforce of the 1980s remained small."[24] Most women who did become employed outside the home entered traditionally female jobs, such as teaching and nursing.

Today, the closed nature of Libyan society prevents outsiders from direct contact with Libyan people, making it difficult to accurately assess women's roles in society. According to Dr. Salma Abd-Al-Jabar, a female member of Libya's General People's Congress, "[As of 2001] women can be found in every career: there are women judges, lawyers, politicians and businesswomen."[25] Dr. Abd-Al-Jabar notes, however, that many women continue to work, as they did in the 1980s, as teachers and nurses.

Other traditional customs have also changed very slowly. Although there have been reports that some young, urban women have begun discarding the traditional veil in favor of Western-style clothes, an American visitor to Libya in 2004

found that most women seen in Tripoli were still veiled.
Some younger, educated city dwellers no longer follow other
traditions such as arranged marriages and living with the
husband's family after marriage, but in rural areas, children
still largely adhere to traditional beliefs and lifestyles. Many
observers think change will eventually come to Libyan society as new generations become more educated and urban-
ized, but they agree that traditional attitudes and practices
among Libyans have so far made that transition for women
a much slower one than Qaddafi advocated.

TRADITION IN LIBYAN CULTURE

Other signs of tradition still at play in Libya include the popularity of traditional food, music, dance, and other forms of
culture. The cuisine of Libya, for example, continues to be
based on a mixture of Arabic, Mediterranean, and Italian
cooking. Typical staples of the Libyan diet include lamb,
chicken, beef, beans, nuts, dried apricots, figs, and unleav-

*A young boy walks with
a tray full of traditional
Libyan dishes to serve to
his family.*

ened bread. Traditional dishes are often stews made of meat and vegetables, served on a bed of couscous (wheat). The most popular drinks, likewise, continue to be traditional sugary tea made from green tea and mint leaves, and thick, black, sweet coffee. Most Libyans also strictly follow Muslim laws that forbid alcohol, pork, and any meat that is not halal (animals that have been slaughtered humanely by a butcher who first says a prayer three times before killing each animal).

Restaurants are few, and most people eat at home, as they always have, with family and sometimes with invited guests. The main meal of the day is usually served at midday, between 1:00 and 3:00 P.M., during a two-hour period in which shops and businesses close for a rest during the heat of the day. A lighter meal is served in the evening. Before eating, Libyans say a short prayer. During meals, women place large platters of food in the center of the table, allowing the men to eat first. People eat with their fingers, but use only the right hand, because the left hand is considered unclean. After eating, Libyans say another prayer and sometimes pass a bowl of perfumed water around the table for cleansing the fingers.

Along with food, traditional folk music and dance remain a top attraction for Libyans. In fact, as the Lonely Planet Web site reports, "The lion's share of Libyan TV is devoted to showcasing various styles of traditional Libyan music."[26] In addition, troupes of folk dancers and musicians travel around the country, performing frequently at weddings and festivals. MSNBC editor and producer Richard Bangs, who visited Libya in 2004, describes one of these performances:

> A local Berber band dressed in black fezzes, red sashes, and white skirts performs a wide whirling-dervishlike performance—spinning about the house; leaping on furniture; balancing vases, apples, and bottles on their heads; and bending over guests like lap dancers so that dinar [the Libyan currency] can be stuffed into their hats. One band member plays an oboe-like *gheeta*, another a drum made of skin stretched over a mortar (a *tende*), a third a flute called a *nay*, and the last a reed and goatskin bagpipe called a *zukra*.[27]

Other popular Libyan traditions also flourish. For example, traditional Libyan artwork and decorative items can be found throughout the country. Influenced by Islamic restrictions

THE BEDOUIN OF FEZZAN

Despite the effects of oil wealth and the Qaddafi revolution, nearly 170,000 Bedouin continue to live in the desert areas of Libya called Fezzan. Virtually all of the Bedouin are Muslim; they speak a local language known as Maghribi; and many still live traditional lives as nomadic shepherds, herding sheep, goats, and camels. The camels are used mainly for transportation, while the sheep and goats are bought and sold. Bedouin families travel into the desert in the winter season and back to the desert's edge during the hot, dry summers. Conditions in this lifestyle are harsh. The Bedouin have no permanent homes but, instead, live in portable, black tents made from woven goat hair. Dairy products—milk, yogurt, and cheese from camels and goats— are their main source of food, supplemented by bread, rice, dates, and on special occasions, meat. Clothing is typically light colored and loose fitting to allow air circulation during the desert heat. Bedouin women work extremely hard, performing most of the labor required for survival. Although some Bedouin men take jobs doing manual labor to supplement their income, many who are used to the nomadic lifestyle consider such work to be degrading. They return to their nomadic life whenever possible.

Traditional Bedouin tents are designed to be portable in keeping with the tribes' nomadic lifestyle.

against realistic depictions of humans or animals, art in the past largely took the form of calligraphy (stylized writing), geometric patterns, and flower motifs. Although modern Libyan painters have embraced realistic themes as well, these traditional motifs continue to adorn craft items such as metalwork, fabrics, rugs, jewelry, and pottery, as well as mosques and public buildings. Tradition is evident, as well, in the popularity of Bedouin-style souks, or markets, where people can purchase many of the same items their grandparents would have bought. Tripoli's old city, for example, has a rich collection of these shops that sell a number of traditional items such as clothing and shoes.

Yet another sign of the importance of tradition for Libyans is their enjoyment of Bedouin pastimes such as horse and camel racing. Horses have been a part of Libyan culture for more than three thousand years, and today Libyans race them or compete in *fantasias*, displays of Arab riding skills. Camel racing is also quite popular. In southern Libya, desert dwellers race a special breed of camel in a sport called *mehari*, in which two riders compete fearlessly, pushing their usually slow-moving mounts to speeds as fast as thirty miles per hour.

The government often subsidizes these traditional activities while outlawing nontraditional influences and restricting Libyans' contacts with the outside world. The result is a culture cut off from many of the Western influences that have penetrated traditional lifestyles in some other Arab countries. Libya therefore remains one of the most conservative Arab societies.

5

SOCIETY AND LIFESTYLE

The influences of oil wealth and Qaddafi's revolution combined to create a prosperous but closed Libyan society in which people were educated, provided government jobs, and given access to free health care and social services. Over the years, however, the economy has crumbled and government policies have left people with reduced prosperity, little freedom, and very limited access to outside goods or stimulation.

EDUCATION, HEALTH, AND SOCIAL BENEFITS

Using increased oil revenues, Qaddafi was able to undertake an ambitious plan of social programs that brought significant improvements to the lives of the Libyan people. Housing, for example, was one of the first of Qaddafi's priorities. At the time of the revolution more than 180,000 families lacked decent shelter. Most poor people lived in rundown hovels and shanty homes ringing the country's larger cities. To remedy this, Qaddafi began a housing project in 1972 that aimed to give every family a place to live by 1982. A massive government spending program succeeded in building 150,000 housing units during the next decade that were provided inexpensively to the poor. By 1986 the government had constructed a total of 277,500 housing units. Many of these units were apartments in high-rise buildings that replaced the shantytowns on the outskirts of Tripoli and Benghazi. Today these buildings still exist and, along with additional housing projects, form the skylines of these and other Libyan cities.

Improving health care was another major goal of the revolutionary government. As a result of the weak health care system, many Libyans in the 1960s suffered from diseases such as typhoid, infectious hepatitis, tuberculosis, rabies, meningitis, malaria, cholera, venereal diseases, and various childhood ailments. With a large infusion of funds, the government within a decade increased the number of doctors from seven hundred to three thousand, more than doubled the number of hospital beds, and created new clinics and health care centers. By 1980 most of the chronic diseases had been wiped out or brought under control. Efforts were also made to provide safe water and improve sewage disposal in order to maintain good health. Today, major public hospitals are located in Tripoli and Benghazi, smaller hospitals or clinics can be found in smaller cities and towns, and mobile health units travel to rural areas. Excellent health care is provided at these facilities at no cost, even to foreign visitors.

Education was also greatly expanded by Qaddafi. Although the monarchy provided Libyans with primary and secondary education, teachers were often foreigners and the quality of the schools was not the best. The new government trained thousands of new teachers, built additional schools, and expanded primary, secondary, and higher education. All education, including college level, was free; students could also attend schools abroad with government funding. These efforts increased school enrollments dramatically, bringing the literacy rate among Libyans from less than 20 percent before the revolution to more than 82 percent in 2004. Today, education is compulsory for ages six to fifteen; thereafter,

Some of the high-rise apartment complexes built by Qaddafi's government loom over a taxi stand in Tripoli.

COMMUNICATION IN LIBYA

Arabic, the language of the Koran (Islam's holy book), is the official language of Libya. Many urban people in Libya, however, also speak English or Italian. In more isolated areas, local tribal languages are still spoken. Libyans typically greet each other with the Arabic phrase "*Salaam aleikum*," (which means "Peace be with you") or "*Sabbahakum Allah bi'l-khair*" ("May Allah give you a good morning"). Another common expression is "*Inshallah*" (meaning "God willing"), used to signal agreement with an idea or to end a conversation. When speaking with Libyans, above all it is important to understand that Libyans highly value courtesy, privacy, and personal honor. Because of this, they often begin their conversations with a series of formal and general questions and answers about their health and families, followed by more in-depth discussion. It is considered extremely rude to criticize another person directly or to discuss family or other very personal matters in public. All conversations in Libya therefore should be kept as polite and respectful as possible.

students may choose to continue their schooling by attending high schools and colleges. Many rural primary schools follow a strict interpretation of Islam and educate girls and boys separately. In most cities, and especially in universities, however, male and female students attend school together.

In the decade following the revolutionary coup, the government also put in place a generous social welfare program. As LaVerle Berry notes, Libya's government bragged in 1977 that "the Libyan social security legislation of 1973 ranked among the most comprehensive in the world."[28] This program included workers' compensation for work-related injuries, retirement benefits, and survivors' pensions to spouses and family members in the event of death. The program also provided food subsidies, employee job protections, income subsidies to the unemployed, maternity leave and child care, orphanages, and old-age homes. Libya's broad social services system remains in effect today, providing aid to all Libyans and protecting them from catastrophic events and risks.

OTHER BENEFITS FROM LIBYA'S OIL WEALTH

In addition to social programs, government spending provided still other benefits for Libyans. Many were given secure, good-paying jobs in Libya's government or in

A large portrait of Qaddafi hangs in a Tripoli school yard to celebrate the Libyan leader's efforts to promote education.

government-owned industries, and wages in all industries were increased dramatically from the days before Qaddafi's coup. Today, the majority of the Libyan population is still employed by the government or government agencies.

The lives of Libyans were also improved by expanded electricity and access to many new consumer goods. Qaddafi's government accomplished a tenfold increase in electrical output from 1970 to 1985 by building both conventional power plants and nuclear facilities. Also, thanks to changes made by the government, most Libyans today own a car and electronic items such as televisions, video recorders, and telephones.

Yet another government benefit was improvement of the country's transportation systems. In 1978, for example, Libya had about fifty-five hundred miles of roads, only about half of which were paved; by 1985 the number of paved roads had increased dramatically to more than fourteen thousand miles. These new roads connected remote villages and oases to urban areas, allowing Libyans to drive and establish bus lines throughout the nation. The government also improved airports and seaports, further expanding Libyans' travel possibilities.

ECONOMIC HARDSHIPS FOR LIBYANS

Although the government provided many benefits, Qaddafi's economic policies soon brought hardships for Libyans. As long as oil income remained high, the government was able to hide many of the economy's problems from the people by simply spending more money. Qaddafi's failure to build thriving businesses was not noticed as long as oil revenues provided workers and their families a comfortable level of prosperity. Economic problems, however, became apparent to the public in the late 1980s and early 1990s when drops in the price of oil and international economic sanctions placed greater pressure on Libya's economy and people. Despite more limited funds, Qaddafi continued to spend massive amounts of money on military armaments and on expensive projects such as the Great Man-Made River Project, further neglecting the economy.

These economic policies have dramatically affected people's lifestyles. Although the country does not release precise data, observers say the government's decreasing revenues have caused cuts in government salaries and jobs, housing and goods shortages, and increased restrictions on travel. In a country where most people work for the government, about 30 percent of Libyans today are reported to be unemployed. For those still employed by the government, wages have not increased in twenty years, and because taxes and the prices of goods have risen, Libyans' purchasing power has declined. As *New York Times* reporter Neil MacFarquhar explained in 2001, "A university professor who used to make the equivalent of $10,800 a year finds the same salary now worth $2,250."[29] Some have estimated the average monthly salary, considering the effects of inflated prices, at only about 250 Libyan dinars, or $83.

Even government benefits such as housing, health services, and pensions have suffered cutbacks. Many contracts for building housing were suspended, for example. Combined with population increases, this is creating yet another housing crisis marked by overcrowding in many of the country's urban areas. Similarly, in the health care field, spending cutbacks have meant that Libya in recent years has lacked vaccines for children, closed mother-and-child health care centers, and done without medicine and qualified personnel needed to treat cancer and heart disease. Libya also has seen recent outbreaks of hepatitis A, polio, and malaria, as well as reports of HIV and AIDS infections.

In addition, the government has been forced to cancel or curtail utility services, construction projects, and agricultural development. This has resulted in problems such as roads with potholes and unreliable telephone service. The cutbacks also have caused the government to incur debts with foreign countries and to expel many foreign workers who it no longer can afford to pay, further disabling the economy. Meanwhile, because the government can no longer pay for students to study abroad, many young Libyans today cannot acquire the technical skills necessary to work in Libya's industries (since these skills are not taught in Libyan schools).

People have also found it increasingly difficult to find the food and goods they need in the government markets. *Wall Street Journal* reporter Barbara Rosewicz, writing in the late 1980s, described the conditions faced by many Libyans: "Tripoli's old 'souk' is like a ghost town; half of the shops have been forced out of business because they can't import perfumes, towels and housewares. Libyans must line up for items like bread, milk and disposable diapers. There was little

Tripoli's old souk (marketplace) remains open, but recent governmental restrictions on imported goods have forced many of the market's vendors out of business.

meat available for months."[30] Only the revolutionary committees and Qaddafi's political leaders were spared food shortages, because the government imported goods for them through special warehouses. The lack of goods for the average person, though, has led to corruption and the surfacing of black markets. These illegal markets, often run by foreigners, provide products otherwise unavailable to Libyans but at greatly increased prices.

To alleviate the shortages, in 1992 Qaddafi began to allow some private-sector merchants to import needed goods. This has created a dual system in which Qaddafi's socialist ideas and private enterprise exist side by side. Free enterprise, however, has only created a widening income gulf between an increasingly prosperous merchant class and poorer Libyans. As reporter Mariam Sami explains,

> In government stores, Libyans line up for subsidized goods like cooking oil, sold for 40 piasters (14 cents) a can, compared to 65 cents in private shops. The average family of six can get a month's ration of flour, cooking oil, sugar, macaroni, tea and tomato paste for the equivalent of $24. Meanwhile, the rich [Libyans] shop in the [private market area], where the main street is lined with brightly lighted markets displaying high-tech kitchen appliances, crystal vases, Mercedes cars and stuffed toys."[31]

Thus, while a few live very well, most Libyans appear to live without great fear of poverty but with very few luxuries.

A CLOSED SOCIETY

The lack of material goods is not the only restriction in everyday life for Libyans. The government of Libya is a strict military dictatorship that limits individual freedoms and Libyans' access to the outside world. According to political commentator Andrew Cockburn,

> For years Libya has been a country largely unknown to the outside world. Even the few outsiders who managed to make their way here usually found it impossible to penetrate beneath the surface. Casual contact between ordinary Libyans and foreigners was heavily discouraged as Qaddafi, who came to power in 1969, gradually imposed

his own brand of revolutionary theory on the country. As embassies closed and foreign companies pulled out throughout the 1970s and '80s, there was an ever diminishing number of visitors from the Western world.[32]

In Libya today there is no free press because the government owns and controls all media. News sources, for example, consist of *Al-Shams*, the main state-run newspaper; JANA, the official government news agency; and numerous smaller news outlets controlled by the government. The government also owns and runs Libyan radio and television stations. All media therefore publish or broadcast only what the government permits. Libyan reporters who participate in satellite television programs, such as those broadcast by the Arabic Al-Jazeera network, have had their Libyan citizenship

LIBYA AND HUMAN RIGHTS

Qaddafi has long been accused of maintaining his hold on power by arresting, jailing, torturing, and causing the "disappearance" of Libyan dissidents. According to the U.S. Department of State's 2003 report of human rights practices in Libya, the country's human rights record remained poor:

> Citizens did not have the right to change their government. Qadhafi used summary judicial proceedings to suppress domestic opposition. Security forces tortured prisoners during interrogations and as punishment. Prison conditions were poor. Security forces arbitrarily arrested and detained persons, and many prisoners were held incommunicado. Many political detainees were held for years without charge or trial. The Government controlled the judiciary, and citizens did not have the right to a fair public trial or to be represented by legal counsel. The Government infringed on citizens' privacy rights, and citizens did not have the right to be secure in their homes or persons, or to own private property. The Government restricted freedom of speech, press, assembly, association, and religion. The Government imposed some limits on freedom of movement.

Despite these types of reported human rights violations and fierce opposition from U.S. and human rights groups, Libya was elected to chair (for one year) the UN Human Rights Commission in 2003. Since then, Libya has released some three hundred political prisoners and allowed human rights groups into the country to observe conditions. However, most analyst agree that only comprehensive reforms will repair Libya's human rights record.

taken away. Government censors also severely edit or prohibit publications or programs that criticize Libya or Qaddafi, threaten Islamic values, or contain Western ideas or perspectives. For example, foreign publications such as *Newsweek* and *Time* are available in Libya, but government authorities routinely censor and sometimes ban them.

Similarly, people in Libya do not have freedom of speech. They have to watch what they say, especially about the government and Qaddafi's leadership. The government even routinely monitors private telephone calls. Teachers in particular must avoid politically sensitive topics. Even at private dinners, people must be careful not to meet or talk with someone considered to be against the government.

Neither are the people allowed to form associations or socialize with whomever they want. Groups where people typically meet to socialize or engage in common interests—such as labor unions, business groups, literary societies, sports clubs, and professional and hobby associations—are banned. Only government-sanctioned political committees are encouraged. Travel, likewise, is restricted by the government, and tourism in Libya, until recently, was virtually nonexistent. Since UN sanctions were lifted in 2003, an increasing number of foreigners have been permitted to visit Libya, but only in groups of three or more, on organized and escorted tours supervised by Libyan guides who try to keep the visitors away from ordinary Libyans.

Qaddafi's regime enforces these restrictions and maintains security through an extensive surveillance system that monitors and controls the activities of individuals. The local revolutionary committees, plus specialized "purification committees" added in 1996, maintain close contact with local communities and look for any speech or activity that might be interpreted as a threat to the regime or a violation of its laws. In addition, the regime maintains several elite military units dedicated to protecting Qaddafi and responding to perceived threats. Anyone suspected of subversive activity is reported to the government, and security forces may arrest, interrogate, imprison, and sometimes even torture or kill these suspects.

Qaddafi's security forces, in fact, have been charged with numerous serious human rights abuses over the years. Human Rights Watch, an international organization that monitors human rights violations, has complained of Libya's "forced disappearance or assassination of political opponents; torture and mistreatment of detainees; and long-term detention without charge or trial or after grossly unfair trials."[33] International pressure has caused Libya to release some of its political prisoners, but Libyan jails reportedly still hold hundreds accused of opposing the government. Qaddafi's control of Libya thus remains absolute, despite occasional outbreaks of civil unrest and rumors of military coup attempts.

LIMITED LEISURE ACTIVITIES

Although little detailed information is available due to Qaddafi's tight controls, Libyans also appear to enjoy little in the way of leisure activities. For example, the state has discouraged or eliminated entertainment spots such as restaurants, bars, and nightclubs as contrary to Islamic values. According to MacFarquhar, the large city of Tripoli has just one nightclub; it is frequented only by men and can play only Middle Eastern music because Qaddafi "barred all Western music in public since the 1980s."[34]

The regime also prohibits most movies and live theater. Qaddafi wrote that "Those who direct the course of life for themselves have no need to watch life working through actors on the stage or in the cinemas."[35] Therefore, only a few films, produced by Arab countries and subjected to careful government screening, are permitted to be shown. In addition, although there are many writers and poets in Libya, the country does not produce many books because of government censorship. Published works cannot express political opinions or disagree with the government. As a result, most books tend to be religious or educational texts, or books that contain praise for Libya and its leadership. Qaddafi's *Green Book*, in fact, is probably the most widely read book in Libya.

Qaddafi even disapproves of and prohibits some sports, such as boxing and wrestling, which he believes are too violent. One tolerated and very popular sport, however, is soccer, known in Libya as football. Boys play informal matches on the streets, and students play in organized teams in schools, from elementary levels to universities. Libya also maintains professional soccer teams that play in Libya and other parts of Africa. In addition, Libya has sent sports teams

Because the Libyan government bans many leisure activities it views as contrary to Islamic values, Libyans typically spend free time with their families.

to the Olympics on several occasions. In the 2000 Olympics, for example, Libyan teams competed in marathon running, judo, and tae kwon do.

In the absence of abundant leisure pursuits, many Libyans content themselves with family activities, picnics on the beaches, and water activities such as swimming, water skiing, and scuba diving. Libya's larger cities are said to have tennis courts, bowling alleys, and golf courses. Perhaps surprisingly, city dwellers in recent years also reportedly have gained access to Internet cafés and satellite television, giving Libyans at least a window to the rest of the world. Internet outlets, however, are restricted. The government has tried to block Internet access to political sites, and signs posted at Internet cafés warn users that political and pornography viewing are strictly prohibited.

Qaddafi's Chaotic Rule

In addition to trying to make ends meet, avoiding trouble with security police, and finding permissible ways to have fun, Libyans have to put up with ever-changing and sometimes unexplainable government policies dependent on the whims of Qaddafi. For example, Qaddafi changed the traditional Islamic calendar that is followed by most Muslim countries. Libya also changed the names of the months of the year, replacing them with names invented by Qaddafi, such as "Bird" (for February) and "Conquest" (for September). Because of these changes, as scholar Mansour O. El-Kikhia reports, "the simple task of determining the day and date has become confusing [in Libya]."[36]

Chaotic conditions also permeate other parts of Libyan society. For example, any action involving government approval or involvement, such as acquiring a birth certificate, can take months or years because of poor administration. Management of utilities is another problem. One Tripoli businessman complained, "[Telephone] billing procedures are virtually non-existent. . . . The only way we know it's time to pay the bill is when the phone is cut off."[37]

Furthermore, Qaddafi is known for making sudden orders and policy changes. Qaddafi's forces often order Libyans to drop what they are doing to report for military service or to attend progovernment demonstrations. These orders routinely disrupt work production and shorten the school day for students. One well-known policy change was a 1977 requirement that every Libyan family raise chickens to achieve self-sufficiency. The government imported scores of chickens and distributed them to families throughout the country. Because of the difficulty of raising chickens in urban apartments, however, many of the chickens were simply eaten. More recently, in 1996 Qaddafi proposed closing all elementary schools so that children could be schooled at home. This proposal, too, proved unfeasible and was abandoned. These types of changing policies and directives make life uncertain and unstable for Libyans.

Although life for many Libyans clearly has been difficult, Libya's actions in recent years, starting with its taking responsibility for the Lockerbie incident in 1999, may signal an opening of its society to the rest of the world. It is still too soon to tell what effects these changes will have on the country, but many hope they will bring a better life for Libya's people.

6

LIBYA'S FUTURE

After transforming Libya into an isolated and struggling nation, Libya's government began showing signs of change in the late 1990s. Qaddafi and many leaders in Libya now appear to recognize the need to improve the country's international reputation and long-term economy. Libya's future may depend on its ability to implement these changes and reinvent itself as a more moderate member of the international community.

LIBYA OPENS ITS DOORS

As the new millennium approached, Libya appeared to be moving rapidly toward political and economic reform. The first breakthrough—Libya's handover of the Lockerbie suspects in 1999—convinced the UN to suspend its economic sanctions on the country. By August 2003, following a trial and conviction of one of the suspects in the bombing, Libya accepted responsibility for the tragedy, stating in a letter to the UN Security Council that it "accepts responsibility for the actions of its officials."[38] In addition, Libya agreed to pay $2.7 billion in compensation ($10 million for each of the 270 people killed) to the families of the victims. These actions led to the formal ending of UN sanctions on September 12, 2003.

Later in 2003, Libya announced it would give up its programs to develop weapons of mass destruction, open its facilities to international inspection, and end its support of international terrorism. Thereafter, Libya quickly welcomed visits by international inspectors and took steps to eliminate its advanced nuclear program and a significant stockpile of chemical weapons. It later agreed to halt military trade with North Korea, Syria, and Iran, all countries considered by U.S. authorities to be involved in developing weapons of mass destruction. Libya's new direction caused the United States to lift the U.S. ban on American travel to Libya and end most U.S. economic sanctions on the country. In a written state-

ment on April 23, 2004, announcing the decision, U.S. officials explained, "Through its actions, Libya has set a standard that we hope other nations will emulate in rejecting weapons of mass destruction and in working constructively with international organizations to halt the proliferation of the world's most dangerous systems."[39] With these developments, U.S. companies once again will be permitted to invest in and send workers to Libya. However, the United States still listed Libya as a "state sponsor of terrorism," a designation that bans goods that might be used for military purposes, prohibits direct air service between the two countries, and freezes Libyan government assets in the United States. These remaining restrictions were lifted by the U.S. government on September 20, 2004

After the initial Libyan reforms, relations between Libya and the West clearly warmed. U.S. special envoy to the Middle East William Burns traveled to Libya to meet with the Libyan government, and for the first time in twenty-four years, the United States in June 2004 reestablished diplomatic relations with the country. British prime minister Tony Blair even flew to Tripoli for a one-on-one meeting with Qaddafi, followed by an April 2004 announcement by Britain that it was ending its support for a European ban on arms sales to Libya. Also in April, Qaddafi visited the European Union headquarters in Brussels—his first visit to Europe in fifteen years. In addition, an increasing number of Western

In 2003 the UN Security Council votes to lift economic sanctions on Libya after Qaddafi accepted responsibility for the bombing of Pan Am Flight 103.

QADDAFI EMBRACES PEACE

Libyan leader Qaddafi, in a statement issued on December 20, 2003, announced that Libya would abandon its weapons of mass destruction and embrace peace. Excerpts of the statement, available on the BBC News Web site, are set forth below:

> In view of the international environment that prevailed during the Cold War and the tension in the Middle East, the Great Socialist People's Libyan Arab Jamahiriyah (GSPLAJ) [Libya's formal name]; has urged the countries in the region to make the Middle East and Africa a region free of the weapons of mass destruction. . . .
>
> Libya has decided, with its own free will, to get rid of these substances, equipment and programmes and to be free from all internationally banned weapons.
>
> It will take all these measures in a transparent way that could be proved, including accepting immediate international inspection. . . .
>
> GSPLAJ believes that the arms race will neither serve its security nor the region's security and contradicts its great concern for a world that enjoys peace and security.

Libya's statement also pledged to limit its missile development to abide by international treaties and agreements to limit the proliferation of nuclear, chemical, and biological weapons.

tourists have been granted visas to visit Libya, and foreign companies are lining up to do business with the country. Observers around the world, in fact, applauded Libya's actions, believing they would return Libya to the world community of nations and pave the way for a better future for the country.

IMPROVED ECONOMIC PROSPECTS

Commentators say Libya is taking these steps toward moderation of its foreign policies as part of a strategy to aid its failing economy. The decades of UN and U.S. economic sanctions, combined with fluctuations in oil prices, took a serious toll on Libya, reducing its ability to import needed technology and other goods and preventing it from selling its products abroad. The sanctions also cut Libya's oil production in half and have prevented much-needed foreign oil investment and exploration in Libya. In addition, experts say Libya may soon face an oil crisis. It has already produced more than half of its known oil reserves, which at expected production levels will be stable only until about the year 2010. Thereafter, experts claim that Libya must find new reserves or face declining oil revenues.

Experts also cite various other problems affecting Libya's economy that stem from Qaddafi's rule. These include a growing population in need of good jobs and better income, a bad work ethic among citizens who have become used to government handouts and nonproductive government jobs, and a lack of technically educated professionals needed to run the oil and other industries. Furthermore, the country is still dependent on foreign labor. Among other concerns are the country's growing water shortage, which threatens agriculture and industry as well as Libya's ability to accommodate its population, and many problems of waste and inefficiency associated with Qaddafi's policies. These types of concerns about Libya's economic future may finally be forcing the country to break out of its isolation.

Libya, in fact, began some economic modernization efforts even before its recent spate of international diplomatic initiatives. Relying on rising oil revenues, the government in 2000 approved a huge five-year investment plan designed to upgrade the country's shattered infrastructure and revitalize its industry. Major planned infrastructure projects include the rehabilitation of ports and harbors, construction of a railway line to the neighboring country of Chad, and a new trans-Libyan highway. Funds will also be allocated to finish the Great Man-Made River Project and to pay foreign debts that accumulated during Libya's economic slowdown. The leader in promoting these economic reforms within Libya is said to be Shukri Ghanem, an economist educated at Tufts University in Massachusetts who is the secretary of the General People's Committee, essentially Libya's prime minister under Qaddafi.

The core of the government's future plan for the economy are twin policies: diversifying the economy to reduce its dependence on oil and encouraging private investment. To accomplish these goals, Libya has already made significant changes to Qaddafi's economic system. For example, the government has removed trade restrictions, ended government and public monopolies on imports, and lowered corporate tax rates. The government has also taken steps to end subsidies for inefficient businesses, to sell government-owned businesses to private buyers, and to encourage competition in the marketplace. At the same time, it has tried to move Libyans out of government jobs and into the employ of private companies. As Ghanem explains, "We have implemented a recruitment freeze in the public sector and are encouraging people to leave the government. Now it's up to the private sector to absorb the excess labour."[40] The government also is aware that it may have to make changes to some of the country's other basic socialist principles, such as its consumer subsidies for food and other staple goods.

In addition, hand in hand with recent diplomatic efforts that have improved relations with the United States, Britain, and other countries, Libya is strongly encouraging foreign investment in its economy. Libya's passage of a new foreign investment law in 1999 and the lifting of UN sanctions, combined with diplomatic efforts, have caused overseas companies to swarm into Libya. Because U.S. sanctions were still in place against American investments until 2004, European oil companies have led the way, seeking mainly to invest in Libya's oil industry. In one project, for example, the Libyan government is relying on foreign help to build a $5 billion pipeline to pump natural gas under the Mediterranean Sea from Libya to Italy. Altogether, as reporter James Badcock explains, "Around 40% of the $35 [billion] of investments due to be made in the period 2003 to 2005, are expected to come from foreign sources."[41]

In recent years, foreign companies have invested heavily in Libya's lucrative oil industry.

American oil companies are also expected to

VISITING LIBYA

In 2004 the United States lifted restrictions on travel to Libya, permitting Americans to travel there for the first time since the 1980s. Although its tourist industry is still undeveloped, Libya is a beautiful country with many interesting sites and places to visit. With its rich history, an enviable location on the Mediterranean Sea, and an interesting desert culture, Libya offers visitors a wide variety of experiences—everything from visiting some of the world's oldest archaeological ruins, to bathing on sun-drenched beaches, to riding on camel caravans across the Sahara Desert. Yet the U.S. government's 2004 travel warning still describes Libya as a dangerous place for American tourists. It suggests that, although Libyan leader Qaddafi has disavowed terrorism, he may still have contact with some terrorist groups. In addition, the warning notes that international terrorist groups continue to plan terrorist attacks against U.S. interests in the region. Visitors, the government says, should be aware of their surroundings, avoid crowds and demonstrations, vary their routines, and in general keep a low profile while in Libya. Anyone considering a trip to Libya is urged to take these security concerns into account.

soon return to Libya, lured by government contracts for oil exploration. Four American companies—ConocoPhillips, Amerada Hess, Marathon Oil, and Occidental Petroleum Corporation—are especially anxious to return to Libya, since they had stakes in the country's oil industry before the imposition of sanctions. Libya is known among oil industry experts around the world as one of the most attractive petroleum investment and exploration sites due to its high grade of oil, its convenient shipping locations, and its vast tracts of unexplored territory. Indeed, Libyan energy minister Fathi Omar Bin Shatwan predicts that the country's total oil reserves "may be more than 100 billion barrels,"[42] more than three times its current known reserves.

Much of the international interest so far has been in the oil industry, but Libya hopes to develop the nonoil sector as well. For instance, the government designated tourism as a top economic priority in its five-year plan. Development of this industry, however, may take time. As Ghanem explains, "Libya has great sites and attractions, [but] the problem is that tourism needs more than that. We still have a lot of work to do regarding visa procedures, hotels and general services."[43] Development of other traditional non-oil industries, especially agriculture and food-related manufacturing, is limited by Libya's shortages of natural resources such as water and arable soil. The manufacturing sector, however, has room for expansion for products such as petrochemicals, aluminum, iron, and steel.

Although the transformation clearly will not happen overnight, and experts say Libya can be expected to remain dependent on oil for years to come, many observers are hopeful about Libya's economic future. Economic reporter Catherine Richards writes, "The ground is indeed being prepared for a major shift in economic activity [in Libya]. It may be some time before Tripoli sports the 10-lane super-highways . . . , but Libya has begun its journey on the road to reform."[44] Successful implementation and management of these economic reforms will perhaps be Libya's most important future challenge.

LIBERALIZATION AND SOCIAL CHANGE

Many analysts believe that a side effect of Libya's economic liberalization will be enormous social changes. Western business-people and tourists are likely to come to Libya as part of the new economic ventures, making it more difficult for the government to discourage contacts between Libyans and Westerners. New businesses may hire Libyan employees, exposing them to new technologies and greater opportunities for travel and contacts outside of Libya. Economic development also may bring renewed prosperity to Libyans, along with increased consumer demands for Western material goods and culture.

Political observers say such changes could pressure Qaddafi to loosen his grip on Libyan society, to allow more individual freedoms and a greater openness to the outside world. Some reports claim that Libyans are already expanding the limits of Qaddafi's isolation. As Associated Press reporter Niko Price explains, "[Libyans] are learning English and using the Internet to chat with relatives in the United States. They watch . . . satellite television. They follow news of European elections, the war in Iraq and the avian flu. They debate democracy and explore international business opportunities."[45] A crackdown by the government, of course, is possible, but such an action might also serve to inflame an already disgruntled public and threaten the economic programs considered so essential to Libya's future.

Libya's modernization, with its Western cultural influences and wealth, may also bring new stresses for traditional culture. Libyans who have found solace in religion and family life during Qaddafi's revolution may find that there are opportunities for a different type of lifestyle, one that offers temptations not found in Libya's conservative culture of the past. Young people, in particular, may be enticed by Western music, clothes, and cars, and perhaps even alcohol and drugs—goods long considered taboo by traditionalists and devout Muslims.

Anecdotal reports from Libya so far, however, indicate that Libyans who have long suffered under Qaddafi's policies are thrilled with the prospects of ending the country's international isolation. Although many Libyans are still cautious about voicing their opinions, a Western reporter found several in early 2004 willing to praise Libya's new direction. Debbie McCully, an American who has lived in Libya since the 1970s, says, "People aren't excited. They're ecstatic." Similarly, Tarek Hassan-Beck, a Libyan oil official who studied in the United States in the 1970s, states, "This political misunderstanding lasted too long, and we're happy these things are taking place." Salah Ibrahim, an economist who heads

A young couple leaves a clothing store in Tripoli. Libyans are beginning to have access to foreign consumer goods.

Tripoli's Academy of Post-Graduate Studies, agrees: "We are not as isolated as before. We are a part of international society. . . . Now we have a new country, and new possibilities to improve ourselves."[46]

Other conservative Arab cultures, such as Kuwait and the United Arab Emirates, have absorbed these types of rapid social and economic changes while still retaining many of their traditions. How both the people and their leaders respond to these pressures in Libya will play a large role in defining the future of Libyan society.

QADDAFI'S FUTURE

Whether Qaddafi can weather these changes and stay in power is yet another looming question. Many commentators suggest that citizen dissatisfaction with his regime has been rising in recent years, but it is impossible to know how many Libyans actually oppose Qaddafi's rule. There is no organized dissent, and because of Qaddafi's highly effective surveillance and security system, most Libyans do not speak out against the regime. A shopkeeper approached in 2004 in Tripoli by a Western reporter, for example, quickly warned, "Don't ask me about politics."[47]

Nevertheless, there are reports of several failed coup attempts in the 1990s, signifying a core of opposition to Qaddafi's policies, particularly within the military. Government security forces attacked and arrested alleged coup plotters in the military in October 1993, resulting in rumors of government torture and executions. In 1996 there were two more coup attempts made by military officers, one of which involved more than forty army officers.

Political analysts claim that the strongest internal opposition to Qaddafi comes from a wave of Islamic militants who have gained strength as a result of a worldwide resurgence of fundamentalist, or conservative, Islam. These include not only religious leaders who have long opposed Qaddafi's reinterpretations of Islamic laws but also organized Islamic groups such as the Islamic Liberation Party, the Islamic Martyrs' Movement, the Libyan Islamic Group, and the Muslim Brotherhood, a group that Qaddafi has battled throughout his rule. All of these groups endorse armed resistance against Qaddafi, and some have been highly successful at recruiting students from Libyan universities and military academies.

According to some observers, the level of Islamist violence in Libya has increased in recent years. In both rural and urban areas, there have been reports of almost daily confrontations between Islamists and police. Qaddafi has also been the target of several assassination attempts. In June 1996, for example, an attack on Qaddafi failed but killed one of his bodyguards. Two years later, members of the Islamic Martyrs' Movement assaulted Qaddafi's convoy near Benghazi, injuring him and forcing him to cancel a rally and a planned trip to Egypt. Some analysts expect this Islamic violence to grow, given Libya's economic problems and Libyans' increasing disappointment with Qaddafi's oppressive, inefficient government. Ray Takeyh, an analyst at the Washington Institute for Near East Policy, for example, suggests the possibility of a military coup followed by a form of Islamic rule: "There is a discernable shift in the mood of the population from reticence to opposition, from passivity to resistance. . . . Post-Qadhafi Libya is likely to be a state governed by military officers who retain a close association with the orthodox Islamic establishment."[48]

Other political observers believe that Qaddafi, now in his sixties, will make every effort to retain control for many more years. Qaddafi apparently has engineered a diplomatic success in recent years with his decision to accept responsibility for the Lockerbie tragedy. This paved the way for the burst

Many Libyans believe that Qaddafi may select one of his two sons, El-Saidi (left) or Mohammed Sayf (right), as his successor.

AISHA QADDAFI

Some observers of Libyan affairs predict that Libyan leader Muammar Qaddafi may select his daughter, Aisha Qaddafi, to succeed him as Libya's head of state. Selecting a woman to lead a conservative Arab country, some say, would be a dramatic decision typical of Qaddafi and would be in line with Qaddafi's longtime support for women's rights. Aisha, in her early twenties and named after Qaddafi's mother, is the Libyan leader's only living daughter (his adopted daughter, Hana, was killed when the United States bombed Libya in 1986).

Aisha graduated from Al-Fatih University in Tripoli with a law degree and has worked to attract investors to Libya's newly developing tourism industry, which many think may signal that her father is preparing her to play a political role. She has also been sent by her father to represent him with other foreign leaders. Frequently seen in designer clothes and sunglasses, Aisha is respected throughout Libya as a model of a successful, modern woman who can work and still abide by Islamic values. If she does succeed her father someday, she will become the first female leader of an Arab country.

A modern woman who also abides by Islamic values, Qaddafi's daughter, Aisha Qaddafi, could conceivably become Libya's future head of state.

of economic activity now emerging in Libya. Qaddafi has even admitted that isolation and some of his past policies have not benefited Libya. These signs perhaps illustrate Qaddafi's adaptability to change, if necessary to secure his regime. As *U.S. News & World Report* writer Thomas Omestad explains, "[Qaddafi has transformed himself] from an eccentric and lethal revolutionary to a more familiar type of Arab [ruler]concerned with easing economic discontent and passing on his rule to kin."[49]

Some expect one of Qaddafi's sons to succeed him in power in the event of his death or a decision to step down as

Libya's leader. His eldest son, Mohammed Sayf al-Islam, is said to be the most likely candidate, but his second son, El-Saidi, may also be a possibility. Sayf, age thirty-one, is studying for a PhD at the London School of Economics and may be in training to take over for his father. He has represented Libya in a number of high-profile political events, including negotiations concerning the Lockerbie settlement. Others suggest that Qaddafi might pick his daughter, Aisha, who reportedly has shown more of an interest in politics than her brothers.

In June 2004, however, reports surfaced of an incident involving Qaddafi that could jeopardize Libya's plans for a brighter future. These news reports suggested that Qaddafi may have been involved in yet another terrorist action, a 2003 covert operation to assassinate the ruler of Saudi Arabia, Crown Prince Abdullah bin Abdulaziz al-Saud, and destabilize his country. Two Libyans—Abdurahman Alamoudi, an American Muslim leader now in jail in the United States, and Colonel Mohamed Ismael, a Libyan intelligence officer in Saudi custody—described the plot to American and Saudi officials. Libya and Saudi Arabia have had a long history of disagreements stemming from Saudi Arabia's friendly relationship with the United States and Qaddafi's claim that the Saudis have funded Libyan opposition groups that want to overthrow Qaddafi. Libya has denied the allegations of its involvement in the assassination attempt, and American officials have begun an investigation. If the allegations are true, such a terrorist plot would contradict Qaddafi's promise to abandon terrorism and possibly lead to a reinstatement of international sanctions on Libya, a situation that could spell disaster for Libya's economic development plans.

Both Qaddafi's and Libya's future, therefore, in the end may depend on Qaddafi's ability to convince the world that he has truly changed his policies. Until this recent news report, many national leaders believed Libya had shown a commitment to moderate its foreign policies and a desire to renew economic relations with other countries. Many people, both in Libya and around the world, still hope that Qaddafi will continue to build on these efforts in order to create the firm foundation needed for Libya's future success.

Facts About Libya

Geography

Location: Northern Africa, bordering the Mediterranean Sea between Egypt and Tunisia

Area: 679,358 square miles (no interior bodies of water)

Area comparative: Slightly larger than Alaska

Border countries: Algeria, Chad, Egypt, Niger, Sudan, and Tunisia

Coastline: 1,097 miles

Climate: Temperate along coast, extremely dry in desert interior

Terrain: Mostly barren, flat to undulating plains, plateaus, and depressions

Natural resources: Petroleum, natural gas, and gypsum

Land use: Arable land, 1.03%; permanent crops, 0.17%; other, 98.8%(1998 estimate)

Natural hazards: Hot, dry, dust-laden *ghibli*, a southern wind lasting one to four days in spring and fall; dust storms and sandstorms

Environmental issues: Desertification; very limited natural freshwater resources; the Great Man-Made River Project, the largest water development scheme in the world, is being built to bring water from large aquifers under the Sahara to coastal cities

People

Population: 5,631,585 (July 2004 estimate), including 166,510 nonnationals

Age structure: 0–14 years, 34.5% (male, 970,026; female, 929,174); 15–64 years, 61.4% (male, 1,744,992; female, 1,630,399); 65 years and over, 4.1% (male, 109,262; female, 115,221) (2004 estimate)

Birthrate: 27.17 births/1,000 population (2004 estimate)

Death rate: 3.48 deaths/1,000 population (2004 estimate)

Infant mortality rate: 25.7 deaths/1,000 live births (2004 estimate)

Life expectancy: Total population, 76.28 years; male, 74.1 years; female, 78.58 years (2004 estimate)

Fertility rate: 3.42 children born/woman (2004 estimate)

Ethnic groups: Berber and Arab, 97%; also Greeks, Maltese, Italians, Egyptians, Pakistanis, Turks, Indians, and Tunisians

Religion: Sunni Muslim, 97%

Languages: Arabic, Italian, and English are all widely understood in the major cities. Literacy rate for those age 15 and over: Total population, 82.6%; male, 92.4%; female, 72% (2003 estimate)

GOVERNMENT

Country name: Great Socialist People's Libyan Arab Jamahiriya; short form, Libya

Form of government: Jamahiriya (a state of the masses) in theory, governed by the populace through local councils; in fact, the U.S. Central Intelligence Agency calls it a military dictatorship

Capital: Tripoli

Administrative divisions: 25 municipalities

National holiday: Revolution Day, September 1 (1969)

Date of independence: December 24, 1951 (from Italy)

Constitution: December 11, 1969; amended March 2, 1977

Legal system: Based on Italian civil law system and Islamic law; separate religious courts; no constitutional provision for judicial review of legislative acts; has not accepted compulsory International Court of Justice jurisdiction

Suffrage: 18 years of age; universal and compulsory

Executive branch: Chief of state: Revolutionary Leader Colonel Muammar Abu Minyar al-Qaddafi (since September 1, 1969) (Note: Qaddafi holds no official title but is the de facto chief of state); head of government: Secretary of the General People's Committee (prime minister) Shukri Muhammad Ghanem (since June 14, 2003); cabinet: General People's Committee established by the General People's Congress

Legislative branch: Unicameral General People's Congress (members elected indirectly through a hierarchy of people's committees)

Judicial branch: Union Supreme Court (judges are appointed by the president)

ECONOMY

Gross domestic product (GDP): $35 billion (2003 estimate); real growth, 3.2% (2003 estimate); GDP per capita, $6,400 (2003 estimate); GDP composition: agriculture, 9%; industry, 45%; services, 46% (2001 estimate)

Labor force: 1.6 million (2001 estimate)

Industries: Petroleum, food processing, textiles, handicrafts, cement

Agriculture products: Wheat, barley, olives, dates, citrus, vegetables, peanuts, soybeans; cattle

Exports: $14.32 billion (2003 estimate)

Imports: $6.282 billion (2003 estimate)

Debt: $4.2 billion (2003 estimate)

Economic aid: $15 million (2000 estimate)

Currency: Libyan dinar (LYD)

NOTES

CHAPTER 1: A DESERT LAND

1. John K. Cooley, *Libyan Sandstorm*. New York: Holt, Rinehart, and Winston, 1982, p. 22.

CHAPTER 2: LIBYA'S MANY CULTURES

2. Geoff Simons, *Libya: The Struggle for Survival*. New York: St. Martin's, 1993, p. 73.

3. Lillian Craig Harris, *Libya: Qadhafi's Revolution and the Modern State*. Boulder, CO: Westview, 1986, p. 4.

4. Quoted in Simons, *Libya*, p. 103.

5. Simons, *Libya*, p. 104.

6. Quoted in Simons, *Libya*, p. 130.

CHAPTER 3: QADDAFI'S LIBYA

7. Muammar Qaddafi, speech broadcast over Libyan radio, September 1, 1969. www.geocities.com/Athens/8744/commun1.htm.

8. Qaddafi, speech.

9. Simons, *Libya*, p. 196.

10. Dirk Vandewalle, ed., *Qadhafi's Libya, 1969–1994*. New York: St. Martin's, 1995, p. 153.

11. Quoted in Simons, *Libya*, p. 215.

12. Mariam Sami, "Gulf Widens Between Average Libyans and Elite; Economy: Falling Oil Prices, Black Market, and the Rise of a Merchant Class Has Frayed Kadafi's Socialism," *Los Angeles Times*, June 9, 1996, p. 4.

13. Quoted in LaVerle Berry, "Historical Setting," in Helen Chapin Metz, ed., *Libya: A Country Study*. Washington,

DC: U.S. Government Printing Office, 1989, p. 57.

14. Khalil I. Matar and Robert W. Thabit, *Lockerbie and Libya: A Study in International Relations*. London: McFarland, 2004, p. 160.

Chapter 4: A Traditional Land

15. LaVerle Berry, "The Society and Its Environment," in Metz, *Libya*, p. 83.

16. Quoted in George Joffe, "Qadhafi's Islam in Local Historical Perspective," in Vandewalle, *Qadhafi's Libya*, p. 145.

17. John Wright, *Libya: A Modern History*. London: Croom Helm, 1982, p. 183.

18. Joffe, "Qadhafi's Islam in Local Historical Perspective," p. 153.

19. Berry, "The Society and Its Environment," in Metz, *Libya*, p. 84.

20. Quoted in Shawky S. Zeidan, "Politics and Government", in Metz, *Libya: A Country Study*, p. 205.

21. Harris, *Libya*, p. 36.

22. Lisa Anderson, "Qadhafi's Legacy: An Evaluation of a Political Experiment," in Vandewalle, *Qadhafi's Libya*, pp. 229–30.

23. Quoted in Mohammed A. El-Khawas, *Qaddafi: His Ideology in Theory and Practice*. Brattelboro, VT: Amana, 1986, p. 98.

24. Berry, "The Society and Its Environment," in Metz, *Libya*, p. 97.

25. Quoted in Delinda C. Hanley, "Women's Rights and Social Affairs Programs Vital to Libya's Progress," *Washington Report on Middle East Affairs*, March 2001, p. 66.

26. Lonely Planet, "Libya Culture," www.lonelyplanet.com/destinations/africa/libya/culture.htm.

27. Richard Bangs, "First into Libya," June 11, 2004. http://slate.msn.com/id/2101814/entry/0.

CHAPTER 5: SOCIETY AND LIFESTYLE

28. Berry, "The Society and Its Environment," in Metz, *Libya,*
    p. 107.

29. Neil MacFarquhar, "Libya Under Qaddafi: Disarray Is the
    Norm," *New York Times,* February 14, 2001, p. A-1.

30. Barbara Rosewicz, "Libyan Tensions Fester Under Qad-
    hafi—U.S. Hopes to Capitalize on Internal Problems,"
    Wall Street Journal, April 14, 1986, p. 1.

31. Sami, "Gulf Widens Between Average Libyans and Elite,"
    p. 4.

32. Andrew Cockburn, "Libya: An End to Isolation?" *National
    Geographic,* November 2000. www.nationalgeographic.com
    /ngm/0011/feature1/index.html.

33. Human Rights Watch, "Libya's Human Rights Record in
    Spotlight: U.N. Commission Needs Membership Crite-
    ria," January 17, 2003. www.hrw.org/press/2003/01/libya
    0117.htm.

34. MacFarquhar, "Libya Under Qaddafi," p. A-1.

35. Quoted in Settlement.org, "Libya: Arts and Literature,"
    www.settlement.org/cp/english/libya/arts.html.

36. Mansour O. El-Kikhia, *Libya's Qaddafi: The Politics of
    Contradiction.* Gainesville: University Press of Florida,
    1997, p. 82.

37. Quoted in Catherine Richards, "Giving Private Business
    the Green Light," *Middle East Economic Digest,* Novem-
    ber 29, 2002, p. 4

CHAPTER 6: LIBYA'S FUTURE

38. Quoted in Associated Press, "U.S. Rewards Libya; Lifts
    Longtime Travel Ban," February 26, 2004. www.ctv.ca/
    servlet/ArticleNews/story/CTVNews/1077807759701_8/
    ?hub=World.

39. White House, Office of the Press Secretary, "United States
    Lifts Majority of Commercial Sanctions on Libya," Bureau
    of International Information Programs, U.S. Department

of State, http://usinfo.state.gov/xarchives/display.html
?p=washfileenglish&y=2004&m=April&x= 200404231520
46ndyblehs8.938015e-03&t=xarchives/xarchitem.html.

40. Quoted in Richards, "Giving Private Business the Green
    Light," p. 4.

41. James Badcock, "Western Firms Scramble for Contracts:
    Western Oil Companies, Including American Majors, Are
    Flocking Back to Libya and Elbowing Each Other Out in
    the Scramble for Lucrative Contracts," *African Business,*
    June 2004, p. 58.

42. Quoted in Egypt Guide, "Libya Reports High Oil Re-
    serves," April 20, 2004. www.egyptguide.net/business/
    showArticle.aspx?CategID=2&ArticleID=40.

43. Quoted in Catherine Richards, "Foreign Firms Make
    Cautious Progress," *Middle East Economic Digest,* No-
    vember 29, 2002, p. 4.

44. Richards, "Giving Private Business the Green Light," p. 4.

45. Niko Price, "Libya Is 'Going with the Flow,'" *Washington
    Times,* May 26, 2004. www.washingtontimes.com/world
    /20040525-093749-1621r.htm.

46. Quoted in Price, "Libya Is 'Going with the Flow.'"

47. Quoted in Thomas Omestad, "Follow the Leader," *U.S.
    News & World Report,* June 7, 2004, p. 28.

48. Ray Takeyh, "Qadhafi's Libya and the Prospect of Islamic
    Succession," *Middle East Policy Council Journal,* Febru-
    ary 2000. www.mepc.org/public_asp/journal_vol7/0002
    _takeyh.asp.

49. Omestad, "Follow the Leader," p. 28.

CHRONOLOGY

A.D.

5th century
The Vandals, a tribe from Spain, invade Libya.

533
The Vandals are defeated by Belisarius, a Byzantine general, and Libya again becomes part of the Roman Empire.

642–652
The Arabs conquer Libya and spread Islam.

16th century
Libya becomes part of the Ottoman Empire.

1911–1912
Italy conquers Libya.

1915
Italy enters World War I, and the Libyan resistance to Italian rule begins under the leadership of a religious group, the Sanusi, leading to a weakening of Italian control.

1931
Italy, under Benito Mussolini, defeats the Sanusi and re-gains control of Libya.

1942
During World War II, the Allies (Britain, France, the Soviet Union, and the United States) oust the Italians from Libya.

1951
Libya becomes independent under King Idris al-Sanusi.

1953
Libya signs agreements of friendship with Britain and the United States.

1956
Libya grants oil exploration rights to two American oil companies.

1959
Major oil reserves are discovered in Libya.

1969
King Idris is deposed in a military coup led by Colonel Muammar Qaddafi.

1970s–1980s
Qaddafi supports various radical insurgent groups.

1970
Libya orders the closure of a British airbase in Tobruk and the U.S. Wheelus Air Force Base in Tripoli; property belonging to Italian settlers is nationalized.

1973
Qaddafi declares a "cultural revolution" calling for the formation of local people's committees.

1977
Qaddafi changes the country's official name from the Libyan Arab Republic to the Socialist People's Libyan Arab Jamahiriya and sets up revolutionary committees to monitor the people's committees.

1981
U.S. president Ronald Reagan begins a campaign against Libyan terrorism, and the United States shoots down two Libyan aircraft that challenge its warplanes off the coast of Libya.

1982
The United States bans the import of Libyan oil.

1986
The United States bombs Libya, killing Qaddafi's infant daughter, and imposes comprehensive U.S. economic sanctions against Libya.

1988
A commercial Pan Am plane is bombed over Lockerbie, Scotland.

1992
The United Nations imposes sanctions on Libya in an effort to force it to hand over for trial two Libyans suspected of involvement in the Lockerbie bombing.

1996–1998
Attempts are made by Libyans to assassinate Qaddafi.

1999
Libya hands over Lockerbie suspects for trial.

2001

A Scottish court in the Netherlands finds one of the two
Libyans accused of the Lockerbie bombing guilty and sen-
tences him to life imprisonment.

2003

Libya is elected chair of the UN Human Rights Commission; Libya agrees to pay $2.7 billion to compensate fami-
lies of the victims of the Lockerbie bombing; the UN
Security Council lifts UN sanctions against Libya; Libya announces that it will abandon its programs to develop
weapons of mass destruction.

2004

The United States lifts the ban on American travel to Libya
and ends most U.S. economic sanctions on the country;
news reports claim that Qaddafi was involved in a plot to
assassinate the ruler of Saudi Arabia.

FOR FURTHER READING

BOOKS

Benjamin Kyle, *Muammar el-Qaddafi*. New York: Chelsea House, 1987. An illustrated biography of Libyan leader Qaddafi.

Lerner Publications, *Libya—in Pictures*. Minneapolis, MN: Lerner, 1996. A young-adult book that examines the topography, history, society, economy, and government of Libya in photographs.

Peter Malcolm, *Libya*. New York: Benchmark, 2004. A young- adult selection that provides an overview of Libya, including geography, history, government, culture, and religion.

Terri Willis, *Libya*. New York: Childrens Press, 1999. Describes Libya's history, geography, economy, culture, people, and religion.

INTERNET SOURCES

Bureau of Consular Affairs, "Libya Consular Information Sheet," http://travel.state.gov/travel/libya.html. A U.S. government Web site that provides practical information and travel warnings for people who plan to visit Libya.

Lonely Planet, "Libya," www.lonelyplanet.com/destinations/ africa/ libya. A popular travel site that provides background on Libyan history and culture, as well as information about tourist attractions and getting around in Libya.

U.S. Central Intelligence Agency, "The World Factbook 2003, Libya," www.cia.gov/cia/publications/factbook/geos/ly.html. A U.S. government site for the CIA that provides geographical, political, economic, and other information on Libya.

WEB SITES

Libya Online (www.libyaonline.com). A Canadian Web site that provides current information about Libya's rich history, arts, music, literature, sports, and natural beauty.

WORKS CONSULTED

BOOKS

John K. Cooley, *Libyan Sandstorm*. New York: Holt, Rinehart, and Winston, 1982. A history of Libya's revolution and modern Libya.

Lillian Craig Harris, *Libya: Qadhafi's Revolution and the Modern State*. Boulder, CO: Westview, 1986. A highly readable analysis of the social, cultural, political, and economic forces that have shaped modern Libya.

Mohammed A. El-Khawas, *Qaddafi: His Ideology in Theory and Practice*. Brattelboro, VT: Amana, 1986. An analysis of Qaddafi's revolutionary theories and their effect on Libya's economy, society, and foreign policy.

Mansour O. El-Kikhia, *Libya's Qaddafi: The Politics of Contradiction*. Gainesville: University Press of Florida, 1997. A study of politics and society under the rule of Qaddafi.

Khalil I. Matar and Robert W. Thabit, *Lockerbie and Libya: A Study in International Relations*. London: McFarland, 2004. A comprehensive history of the Lockerbie incident and its resolution.

Helen Chapin Metz, ed., *Libya: A Country Study*. Washington, DC: U.S. Government Printing Office, 1989. An overview of the geography, history, economy, society, and politics of Libya prepared by the U.S. Library of Congress.

Geoff Simons, *Libya: The Struggle for Survival*. New York: St. Martin's, 1993. A history of modern Libya with an emphasis on Libyan-U.S. relations.

Dirk Vandewalle, ed., *Qadhafi's Libya, 1969–1994*. New York: St. Martin's, 1995. A collection of essays about modern Libya written by political science professors and researchers.

John Wright, *Libya: A Modern History*. London: Croom Helm, 1982. A well-known history of Libya and Qaddafi's revolution.

PERIODICALS

James Badcock, "Western Firms Scramble for Contracts: Western Oil Companies, Including American Majors, Are Flocking Back to Libya and Elbowing Each Other Out in the Scramble for Lucrative Contracts," *African Business*, June 2004.

Delinda C. Hanley, "Women's Rights and Social Affairs Programs Vital to Libya's Progress," *Washington Report on Middle East Affairs*, March 2001.

Neil MacFarquhar, "Libya Under Qaddafi: Disarray Is the Norm," *New York Times*, February 14, 2001.

Thomas Omestad, "Follow the Leader," *U.S. News & World Report*, June 7, 2004.

Catherine Richards, "Foreign Firms Make Cautious Progress," *Middle East Economic Digest*, November 29, 2002.

———, "Giving Private Business the Green Light," *Middle East Economic Digest*, November 29, 2002.

Barbara Rosewicz, "Libyan Tensions Fester Under Qadhafi—U.S. Hopes to Capitalize on Internal Problems," *Wall Street Journal*, April 14, 1986.

Mariam Sami, "Gulf Widens Between Average Libyans and Elite; Economy: Falling Oil Prices, Black Market, and the Rise of a Merchant Class Has Frayed Kadafi's Socialism," *Los Angeles Times*, June 9, 1996.

Patrick E. Tyler, "Two Are Said to Tell of Libyan Plot to Kill Saudi Ruler," *New York Times*, June 10, 2004.

INTERNET SOURCES

Samia Amin, "Recent Developments in Libya," Carnegie fact sheet, February 10, 2004. www.ceip.org/files/projects/npp/resources/Factsheets/developmentsinlibya.htm.

Amnesty International, "Libya: Time to Make Human Rights a Reality," April 26, 2004. www.amnestyusa.org/countries/libya/document.do?id=80256DD400782B8480256E7F00555CBD.

Arab Net, "Tripoli: The Old City," 2002. www.arab.net/libya/la_oldtripoli.htm.

Associated Press, "U.S. Rewards Libya; Lifts Longtime Travel Ban," February 26, 2004. www.ctv.ca/servlet/ArticleNews/story/CTVNews/1077807759701_8/?hub=World.

Richard Bangs, "First into Libya," June 11, 2004. http://slate.msn.com/id/2101814/entry/0.

BBC News, "Libyan WMD: Tripoli's Statement in Full," www.geocities.com/Athens/8744/mylinks1.htm#.

Bethany World Prayer Center, "The Fezzan Bedouin of Libya," 1997. www.ksafe.com/profiles/p_code1/2002.html.

Andrew Cockburn, "Libya: An End to Isolation?" *National Geographic*, November 2000. www.nationalgeographic.com/ngm/0011/feature1/index.html.

Egypt Guide, "Libya Reports High Oil Reserves," April 20, 2004. www.egyptguide.net/business/showArticle.aspx?CategID=2&ArticleID=40.

Galen R. Frysinger, "The Man-Made River, Libya," www.galenfrysinger.com/man_made_river_libya.htm.

Human Rights Watch, "Libya's Human Rights Record in Spotlight: U.N. Commission Needs Membership Criteria," January 17, 2003. www.hrw.org/press/2003/01/libya0117.htm.

Ibrahim Ighneiwa, "Libya: Mohammad 'Idris I' al-Sanousi King of Libya [1951–1969]," http://ourworld.compuserve.com/homepages/dr_ibrahim_ighneiwa/idris.htm.

Infoplease, "Qaddafi, Muammar al-," www.infoplease.com/ce6/people/A0840668.html.

Libya Online, "Libya," 1997–2004. www.libyaonline.com/libya.

Lingnet, "Libya: History, Religion, and Resources," http://wrc.lingnet.org/libyahis.htm.

Lonely Planet, "Leptis Magna," www.lonelyplanet.com/destinations/africa/libya/attractions.htm.

———, "Libya Culture," www.lonelyplanet.com/destinations/africa/libya/culture.htm.

Middle East Times, "Aisha Qadhafi Favored to Succeed Her Father," 2000. www.metimes.com/2K/issue2000-49/reg/aisha_qadhafi_favored.htm.

Khelwat El-Mrabit, "Al-agailla Concentration Camp (a poem)," www.libyana.org.

Natural History Museum of Los Angeles County, "Artwork Shows How the Sahara Changed," www.nhm.org/africa/tour/desert/011.htm.

New Dawn, "The River of Life," July/August 2001. www.newdawnmagazine.com/articles/The_River_Of_Life.htm.

Niko Price, "Libya Is 'Going with the Flow,'" *Washington Times*, May 26, 2004. www.washingtontimes.com/world/20040525-093749-1621r.htm.

Muammar Qaddafi, speech broadcast over Libyan radio, September 1, 1969. www.geocities.com/Athens/8744/commun1.htm.

Nigel Richardson, "Libya for Beginners," April 10, 2004. www.telegraph.co.uk/travel/main.jhtml?xml=/travel/2004/04/10/etlibya100404.xml.

Settlement.org, "Communicating with Libyans." www.settlement.org/cp/english/libya/commun.html.

———, "Libya: Arts and Literature," www.settlement.org/cp/english/libya/arts.html.

———, "Libya: Sports and Recreation," www.settlement.org/cp/english/libya/sports.html.

Ray Takeyh, "Qadhafi's Libya and the Prospect of Islamic Succession," *Middle East Policy Council Journal*, February 2000. www.mepc.org/public_asp/journal_vol7/0002_takeyh.asp.

United Nations Educational, Scientific, and Cultural Organization, "The Great Man-Made River Project," 2001. www.unesco.org/water/ihp/prizes/great_man/gmmrp.shtml.

U.S. Department of State, Bureau of Consular Affairs, "Travel Warning: Libya," June 28, 2004. http://travel.state.gov/travel/libya_warning.html.

U.S. Department of State, Bureau of Democracy, Human Rights, and Labor, "Libya: Country Reports on Human

Rights Practices—2002," March 31, 2003. http://us.polit info.com/Information/Human_Rights/country_report_0 89.html.

U.S. Department of State, Bureau of Public Affairs, "Background Notes: Libya," July 1994. http://dosfan.lib.uic.edu/ ERC/bg notes/nea/libya9407.html.

White House, Office of the Press Secretary, "United States Lifts Majority of Commercial Sanctions on Libya," Bureau of International Information Programs, U.S. Department of State, http://usinfo.state.gov/xarchives/display.html?p =washfile-english&y=2004&m=April&x=20040423152046 ndyblehs8.93 8015e-03 &t=xarchives/xarchitem.html.

INDEX

PICTURE CREDITS

ABOUT THE AUTHOR

Debra A. Miller is a writer and lawyer with a passion for current events and history. She began her law career in Washington, D.C., where she worked on legislative, policy, and legal matters in government, public interest, and private law firm positions. She now lives with her husband in Encinitas, California. She has written and edited publications for legal publishers as well as numerous books and anthologies on historical and political topics.